FOR THE RECORD

the book of
rock n' roll afterlife

channeled by

Deborah Burns

BALBOA.
PRESS
A DIVISION OF HAY HOUSE

Balboa Press books may be ordered through booksellers or by contacting:

Balboa Press
A Division of Hay House
1663 Liberty Drive
Bloomington, IN 47403
www.balboapress.com
1-(877) 407-4847

Cover design:
Daniel Lim, Houston, Tx.

ISBN: 978-1-4525-7659-6 (sc)
ISBN: 978-1-4525-7660-2 (e)

Library of Congress Control Number: 2013911000

Printed in the United States of America.

Balboa Press rev. date: 07/23/2014

Table of Contents

Table of Contents

Introduction

by Jehovah Eloah Va Daath . . .

World cultures-as they are today—are a form of idol worship. The idols of the 21st century are thought to be very different from those of primitive tribes or the civilizations of antiquity . . . but are they truly *that* different?

Sports figures, TV and movie personalities, musicians, authors, painters, politicians-these are the focus of the limelight bestowed by media moguls and lustily consumed by readers and viewers living vicariously through these larger than life people-hereafter referred to as *'Iconic People'*.

The Iconic People are the object of desire, jealousy, envy and admiration and marketing wizards know how their endorsement of a product, service or event is the New Age version of the *Midas touch.*

The sword of power that is wielded by the Iconic People does have two edges-a positive as well as a negative. Some who wear the mantle of their celebrity and influence comfortably do use it to support a cause, fashion look, genre' of music or art . . . maybe just bring a philosophic, spiritual or esoteric concept to the public's attention.

Look how Hollywood has embraced Scientology, the Mystical Quabbalistic teachings, Meditation of different sorts and Yoga in its various disciplines. All got their big media push into public awareness from celebrities lending their star power behind them.

Thinking back a few decades, there were musicians and scholars, actors and activists standing shoulder to shoulder with Dr. Martin Luther King, Jr. in the days of Civil Rights struggles and demonstrations. The same scenario happened with Apartheid in South Africa, human rights in Tibet, China and other areas of the world-a pattern we've seen repeat itself often because the formula has proven to be so effective. The *Iconic People* have been thrust to the forefront of mass consciousness to point the way for the general public. This phenomenon is now a global one with the arrival of the instantaneous electronic data bridge

<u>Here is the purpose of this book</u>: to explain how spirituality works as it applies to reincarnation, pre-incarnation, "contracts" and delivering messages into the Earth plane that propagates Unconditional Love and the teachings of The Way. The information will be presented by some guest presenters whose names will be familiar to most readers. Some volunteered and some were personally invited by me to add their voice and experience to this presentation.

Let's start at the beginning and review and address some of the basic tenets of The Way; by doing so, we will get our collective thinking all moving in the same direction.

Many of you may not be familiar with the term: "The Way". It refers to the teaching of Jesus the Christ during his brief ministry in Galilee and surrounding areas. Followers of Jesus were called *"Followers of The Way"* for decades before the term *"Christians"* came to be used. The basis of this philosophy is simple:

- *Love God with your heart, mind, soul and spirit*
- *Love your neighbor as yourself*
- *See the beauty in all things*

Essentially these 3 rules supersede the 10 Commandments of the Old Testament; they are all about Unconditional Love.

If your heart tempo changes or your stomach tightens into a ball at the mention of the word _reincarnation,_ you have lots of kindred spirits-at least in the Western Hemisphere. It's been estimated that approximately two-thirds of the current world population embraces the concept of rebirth . . . perhaps the concept is worth a closer look.

The over-simplified explanation of the process goes as follows:

Souls dwell in an area called _"The Guff"_ located in the etheric world. Souls are pure energy bits that come directly from the thought and will of the Creator (known by many names). Souls have lessons they need to learn to fulfill their purpose for being-i.e. why they were created. There is an endless array of lessons that fall into this category . . . but they all have something to do with love. The soul decides that it needs a particular experience to learn a specific lesson. A request is submitted to the Grand Council which consists of the Elohim (sort of a _Council of Creators_) and the Brotherhood of Light (sort of a _Board of Directors_). The concept logistics and plan for executing the project are reviewed and discussed thoroughly and approval is given or not.

The soul has to enlist the co-operation of other souls who agree to assist in the venture. There are lots of parts to cast-birth parents, siblings, nemeses/protagonists, spouses and key players who will figure prominently at key points along the path of the life. The process might be loosely compared to casting and preproduction for planning the making of a movie.

Once the plan is approved and all the players are set, the next step is the Contract. This is the solemn agreement between the Soul and God as to the terms and details of the plan and how it is to be done and within which parameters . . . also the consequences if the obligations are not met.

All the aspects are agreed to and understood before the "launch" of the project. A key component is the choice of birth parents as the source of the correct DNA for optimum physical components of the project. [YES-they are chosen by YOU beforehand] Sometimes they are selected for help launching the youngster, sometimes as a hurdle that must be overcome to reach one's potential and destiny.

It is essential to understand this concept:

You are a SPIRITUAL BEING having a PHYSICAL experience . . . not a PHYSICAL BEING having a SPIRITUAL experience. The two are very different and you must learn to make the distinction in your mind. This awareness makes living your life experiences so much easier. Not understanding this or losing sight of it can create many unnecessary challenges.

Occasionally a specific Soul Person is chosen for a specific assignment-more often, a call goes out for volunteers for a particular project and the best suited candidates are chosen from the pool of volunteers.

Once the soul enters the body of the infant-it has up to three days of birth to do so—it is "launched" into the Earth plane. It might surprise you to know that as a rule, we do not intervene unless invited or asked to do so. Many times we have to patiently wait for you to 're-discover' us so you'll know to ask us for help, guidance and protection-only then can we lavish lots of it upon you! This hands-off policy is completely the epitome of Unconditional Love, believe it or not. It was set in place by the Ancient Ones in the *Before Times*-during the Creation process. It has now become *standard operating procedure*, so to speak. Intervention without invitation is regarded as interference. It is not allowed.

As the newly-arrived person makes their way through their physical journey and experiences all the soul lessons they come to learn, if they choose to develop their spiritual self and the abilities and capabilities contained therein, at some point they get to have their *quickening*. A *quickening* is achieved when the person makes a reconnection with their Soul Self (or Higher Self) and their spiritual 'switchboard' lights up and begins to function in earnest. At that point it's GAME ON! Gifts and abilities and awareness that had been resting in a state of dormancy suddenly become operational to you. It can take many forms: ability to 'hear' your guidance or to channel, perhaps you can see the aura colors that surround people, maybe your 6th sense gets very strong and very accurate if you listen to it . . . it's different for each person.

Throughout the life path, the person shapes their destiny by the decisions and choices they make every minute, every hour, every day-week-month and year throughout their timeline. Free will and the freedom to choose is HUGE in the Soul's journey-but the general storyline of the CONTRACT stays in place.

As background information: it's useful to know that self-medicating to 'numb-out' is used for two possible outcomes:

a. to put distance between Self and God
b. to attempt to close the gap and get much closer to God

think back to people in your past that chose the drug or alcohol path—maybe it was you. Sometimes they wanted to have their spiritual epiphany and God vision; sometimes they were running away as fast and as far as possible.

OK. Your life on the physical plane is rolling and soon it's time to exit stage left and return back to the place from whence you came. In large part that's also determined by yourself. Age and exit strategy is generally set forth in your Contract; outcomes can be altered in some cases, but usually it just goes by the script.

After transition, there is an orientation time; reunion with loved ones, time in the reorientation chamber (known to all Guff residents as the "pink room") if needed for reintegration into the etheric way of doing things and processing emotional carry-over from your time in the physical Earth plane. It gets its pink color from the intensity and purity of Divine Love energy that is present there. It is derived directly from God/the Elohim. Pink is the color of that specific specialized energy frequency. The pink energy is denser than other frequencies . . . more like a heavy fog consistency than the types of energy to which you are accustomed. It is an area that is reserved for this important aspect of returning 'home'. There is also the option to assist others' transition if you choose to do so. Once the process is completed, if you wish to do so, you can set about the planning of your return engagement back to the Earth plane, but only if you should so desire . . . some choose to wait a while; some elect to never return.

Obviously, I skipped a lot of details as I described the life process from the spiritual vantage point. There is LOTS more to it, and it all happens more rapidly than it sounds, but this synopsis sets the stage for the channeling that is to follow. If you want to know more about it, go to the website: www.divinewayoflife.com.

About who is speaking . . . I am *Jehovah Eloah Va Daath*-essentially I am Mother God, the counterpart to *Jehovah Elohim*-Father God. We are parts of the greater group referred to as The Elohim. I have been intricately involved in the events of the Earth plane since its inception and had a very prominent role in its creation and history-both the past and what lies ahead in the future. My devotees refer to me as Elle (*Ellie*). This project is my idea and the information that Deborah is putting forth is hand-picked and chosen and edited by ME as well as those who asked to participate. It has been provided with special protection from any negative influence from the Dark Side. All that you read here is Divine Truth.

That is all for this portion.

—Elowah

Deborah sends greetings . . .

I am about to present the results of channeling twelve separate entities that have interesting and valuable information to share with you. They will be familiar names for the most part, but you'll be introduced to some new names too . . . especially in the introduction as you read the back story for this book.

The Divine Family will be collaborating on this work they want to call: **For the Record**. By channeling the entities directly, I am presenting the direct words and impressions of some Iconic People who have made transition.

Some of these individuals have arbitrarily chosen to visit me earlier-either in meditation or channeling or speaking to me directly. Usually communication is done in words-either spoken (internal) or written (so-called "automatic").

It will not be my words that you will be reading, but theirs; their description, their language, their experience, their message back to us from where they are now—virtually unplugged and unedited. It's conversational in its form, so those of you who are sticklers for proper grammar and syntax, please relax your standards for a minute and focus your attention on the content of the concepts. My challenge was to put their words into a format that is easy to read and capture the truest essence of the message that's here for you. You will notice that some statements are very similar and certain key points overlap. As I stated earlier, I wrote it all down as they presented it-repeats too. I viewed the overlaps as confirmation of definitive Universal Divine Truths.

Some may think the material presented here could be labeled as '**gnostic**" (defined as 'hidden or secret knowledge') or '**mystical**" (defined as 'Divine Truth that comes directly from God to selected recipients') or a combination of both. I leave that label determination to the reader. I know the information came to me directly from the sources (i.e. individual contributors) at the personal invitation of Jehovah Eloah Va Daath. I found the narratives to be articulate and thoughtful, not to mention fascinating and insightful. The energy of each person was completely different and unique as they transmitted their messages to and through me.

. . . So let me introduce to you: *For the Record*.

Deborah Burns

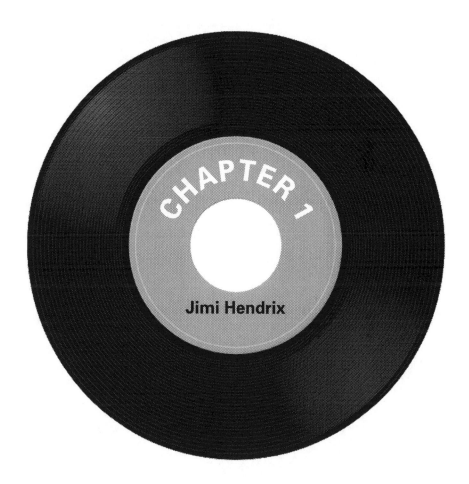

CHAPTER 1

Jimi Hendrix

Jimi Hendrix

It's been like such a long time by Earthly time standards since I got to speak my mind from the heart. It feels so amazing . . . ! What a great opportunity to talk about some things I've learned.

First, I must say I realized my lifelong wish when I was there making my music-letting the sounds and the new music contained in them pilot me through my life journey. All I created was not created by me . . . a lot was channeled to me and through me, but only when I learned to slip into *The Zone*. I called it getting *"zoned out"*. Most people thought I meant drug induced "zone", but it was the music of the Cosmos. Sometimes I did drugs to quiet all of it down for a short time so I could clear my head and rest some 'cause the flow of the music was relentless . . .

I heard it non-stop every waking moment and in my dreams at night. I always kept my guitar close at hand 'cause I knew I would have to play something that was coming through: lyrics-words, had to be written down, but the true song I could recall and play anytime-even changing it up a different way each time.

The pool of talent-the sheer numbers of players, singers, songwriters of the highest caliber imaginable-I cannot explain or describe it with written words. The idea of *"For the Record"* oversimplifies the reality, but gives your mind something and somewhere to start to comprehend.

It's all so beautiful . . . ! It's all love and harmony without a beginning or end; it's colors and vibration; it's all infused with universal love that links us all together on a level most folks don't even feel or even realize.

We no longer need physical maintenance like sleeping, eating, smoking, sex, pee breaks . . . Bet you have no idea how much of 3-D Earth time is used up by that kind of stuff. Shopping, laundry, watching TV, talking on the phone, arguing—Man, so much time and energy really wasted. I can truly say with certainty-don't miss much about it by comparison.

I said one time that "when I die, just let them play my records". I wanted my music to be remembered. That was 3 generations ago and counting. Those kids at Monterey and Woodstock are grandparents now and their grandkids are asking for guitars for their Christmas or birthday gifts-just like I asked my Dad-cause they want to play some song they heard that won't stop playing in their head. Play it, express it, accept it like a gift, honor it or lose it. There's a time element to the process, you know . . .

Talking about time-maybe you'd like a little history so you'll get a clearer picture of my reality:

I have been "*nobodys*" and I have been "*somebodys*" and many of both. I have been every race and color and in most major civilizations. Sure, you've read about some things I did in history books and seen some stuff shown in movies. My name, my identity is not important. What I need to tell you is this: building stone monuments to glorify one's time on Earth is almost comical 'cause it cannot last—never will. It cannot withstand the elements beating away at it decades after centuries, after eons-and it fades in people's memory. Mental and spiritual stuff, that's what lives through the ages. It lives on because you have touched people's hearts in some way. It's how you make people feel, how you express what's rattling around inside your own head and heart and soul, how you preserve that expression-that's what endures. It's the love thing, pure and simple . . . so simple it's fantastically profound; that's the true definition of soul and soul music . . . even James Brown agrees with that!

I don't think it would be too cool to like name drop-like I was so and so and did this and that . . . that's an ego thing and so removed from all that is here where I am now. That past scene-all the different identities, accomplishments and failures over all the centuries-all shaped my soul essence for what I do now.

New arrival guys are always saying, "Hey Jimi, when you going back to finish what you started?" I usually grin and say nothing-just strum my guitar. I'll tell you why: my Earth trip had a beginning, a middle and an end just like a book, speech or a song. Nothing to prove, nobody to impress . . . I like to think-and I'm told by some here-that I opened up minds to new possibilities. My technique was *no* technique. I played 'til the guitar felt like another limb on my body. I kept at it 'til my fingers knew how to bring out the sounds in my subconscious. My music was like my personal private religion . . . just God and the music and me. I was pleased and usually surprised (in a good way) when the people hearing me play received it and actually 'heard' it in the spirit in which I offered it to them. It wasn't always the case, you know . . . but when it was, it was cosmic magic!

My death wasn't glorious, my life wasn't really glorious, but both accomplished something that will last a really long time. My death was a stepping stone: to step back to where I belong. My life was really a bridge to connect the beginning to the end. Guess that in one way or another I always end up building structures of some kind . . .

I have the capability and the ability to play through some people in the form of channeling . . . those who will welcome it and allow it. I'm very respectful about it. Helps me keep my 3-D chops up-you know?

One thing I do kinda' miss sometimes . . . when I was on those big stages and the energy of all those kids listening to me play was zeroed in on me like a heat seeking missile. Man, talk about a high . . . ! Words can't describe it-you just gotta feel it sometime. The buzz lasts for days.

I think it's so ironic . . . all those who say they love Jimi Hendrix or his music or a particular song-then and now. Truth is I had some people who loved me and whom I loved along the way, but the inner core group was pretty small. Whatever gaps and voids I felt in that regard-God helped me fill with music energy; that was something I learned when I got here . . .

People, in general, were different when they depended on their ears and imagination for most of their entertainment-like our grandparents listening to radio programs like *Grand Ol' Opry*, etc.—before TV; that is why I think the public's support of musicians, bands, radio stations and record labels has endured. Remember when you were a kid and bought a new album? You'd lie on your bed or the couch or floor and read and re-read the liner notes and lyrics while you listened to the artist—right? Your imagination became engaged while your ears were hearing the sounds and your brain was translating the vibrations for the consumption of your subconscious.

There are a few shining stars about to explode on the music scene in the very near future. In the 1960's, the scene was split between the U.S. and British/London markets. Now with the social network thing available to every garage band, front porch picker and shower singer—everything is global. The scene is global. Your message, energy, vibe (positive or negative) can be in everybody's face worldwide within 1 week or less. We hope you use your super powers for good! Oh yeah . . . use your imagination as much as you can.

There's a lot of work to do in your world—it's like trying to turn a herd of stampeding cattle away from some dangerous situation in the trail ahead. If you're reading this, I know you're looking for some answers 'cause you got lots of questions. It's the seekers who will inherit the bulk of the workload to be done. Step up, join up, speak up, crank it up.

Find your voice and use it—but could you do an old friend a favor? Know what you're talking about, speak the truth and do it with love; that's how to change the world.

Thanks for listening . . . maybe I'll get to do this again. Peace . . .

Jimi

9-22-10 [Jimi Hendrix continues]

Hey—I got another turn to speak about some pretty heavy things that have been on my mind . . .

Let's talk about guitars. As I said, I kept practicing 'til mine felt like another part of my body. I had a few that were special and several were 'sacrificed' onstage like in Monterey. That whole burning-the-guitar was a spontaneous action, but it was a true sacrifice. In the Old Way when you achieve a goal that's been long sought after, a sacrifice is offered as an acknowledgment and act of appreciation.

I guess my white Strat was my main instrument-most visible because of the Woodstock movie and event too, of course. It had a special harmonic quality that I thought sounded like singing. That voice characteristic was one of the reasons I wanted to play the *Star Spangled Banner* on it . . . I thought it would be really beautiful-and it was. Carlos Santana has a Gibson with the unique singing voice quality to it. The harmonics resonate so completely within the wood; the whole instrument vibrates, not just the particular string. I played lots of different guitars: cheap ones that couldn't stay in tune and expensive ones with no soul and certainly no connection to my soul. The axe has to be right for everything to flow smoothly. Young guys (and girls too) are always asking what guitar, what strings, what pick-ups, what string height to the fretboard . . . there's no way answer these questions. Man, it's your hands and your ears that choose these things-not your brain or reading a book or hearing a quote in some interview. When you feel the magic start to flow . . . it's right.

When I was coming up as a player, I really loved to talk to the old blues cats-guys who lived the blues before they played the blues . . . before it was cool or hip. *"Play your pain, play your frustration, play your loss and disappointment,"* they would say. Lots of players do-most do not. Stevie Ray Vaughn played from his guts, from his bones. He was exceptional. We hang together here some and talk about lots of things. Robert Cray, Buddy Guy, Bonnie Raitt, Eric C., B. B., Carlos and many others-plus the old guys like Muddy Waters and Robert Johnson-the players whose records you heard as you grew up. Man, they really influenced lots of kids just starting out. A little known fact is that the British Invasion was largely influenced by the old blues masters of the American South.

All the familiar faces . . . they're all working out soul stuff-lifetimes of it. Think about this: Blues are a way for the soul to work out really deep emotions, then they don't have so much to process on the other side (here). Emotions-good and bad, great or small—require processing once you arrive here. There are people who help you and special areas you can go-like a retreat-where you can work out stuff that followed you here in your heart. If you *'twist and shout and work it on out'* while you're in your body, it all goes so much better as you re-orient to this world and its parameters. Lots of the greats were black players who pulled from their experiences to inspire their version of the blues, but they didn't have a monopoly on hard times, hard knocks, plans that failed, love that didn't last-lots of white artists too-again, Stevie Ray is a good example . . . Amy Winehouse too . . . and, of course, the artists who contributed to this book.

The genre' of blues is somewhat unique in the way it's useful in processing emotion. What about other genre's? Rap, Metal, Country, Folk, Classical, Jazz, Punk, Glam, Pop and each increment of each type of sound-all have a unique bandwidth of energy contained within it . . . that explains in part why each genre' attracts a particular type of listener.

Some listeners like to hear all kinds of music. A guy who's all about Miles Davis jazz is in a very different place emotionally and mentally than someone who's losing their mind at a Journey, Queen or Zeppelin concert. The bands of energy fill and compliment those present within the individual people. This also explains why some music completely turns on one person and shuts down the guy next to him. HE likes Black Sabbath and Robin Trower, SHE can't listen to enough Barry Manilow and James Taylor. Worlds apart genre's within the same topic of music. Do you see?

The vibe of the 60's artists and into the 70's was gentler, more innocent in a way. After disco came and went, everyone started sharing their anger and angst with their audiences *without* the love thing. It was hard-edged and brute forced and some came right out of my hometown-Seattle-that whole scene called 'grudge'. Big shifts are like taking the pulse of a generation with double bass drum kicking the tempo.

Music is like a pen: both extremely powerful tools capable of so many applications. It can put a baby to sleep or stir a crowd to their feet in a frenzy; worship God and celebrate Love or conjure up *Sympathy for the Devil*—it's a complete spectrum. You follow my thoughts on this? It gives a voice to those without one; it takes down the barriers between people. African tribes or a crowded disco dance floor—all kinds of people sharing an experience because of the frequency band of the energy present. It's all one heartbeat of God. Man breaks it up, speeds it up or slows it down . . . Man does that.

When a Native American sits on a rock and chants a prayer song or plays his flute, he is extending himself in an effort to reconnect with God-or whatever he calls the Force greater than himself. Is it any different for a fourteen year old boy sitting in his bedroom learning the licks to *Stairway to Heaven* or *Smoke On The Water*?

There's always some cats looking for some kind of short-cut to fame and riches. More than one followed up on the legend about the Crossroads and making a deal with the Devil. It goes something like: "I will guarantee you'll realize all your dreams-fame, wealth, success, **IF** you'll pledge your soul to me." I've heard old guys talk about it-maybe even knew someone who made the trade. More guys chased after it than you might imagine. It was possible but the consequences do not justify the momentary gain. In the end, if you ask, God voids the contract and the Enemy goes home empty handed and grumbling . . .

Broke, needy, hungry and frustrated artists make great candidates for the Dark Side to attempt to work their program. What they offer is sweet and tempting-sounds too good to be true, but the guys don't bother to read the fine print of the deal. The price is steep. Fortunately, God has the ultimate loophole.

Once in a generation or someone's lifetime, all the aspects get right: the stars align, the planets are right, the space and time junction is spot on, all the pieces fit, the melody and lyrics are just right, the instruments and voices are harmonious and the energy of the players mesh—that's when it's MAGICAL.

Those moments are even caught on tape sometimes-sometimes not. It's just a happening for those present. [I always taped everything when I was in the studio.] When it happens, those are the rock n' roll memories people debate and discuss for decades. That's how legends are made . . . that's history being made. Some people found a new way to think about a finite number of notes on a scale; added bass, drums-maybe a keyboard and vocals. It's the true rock n' roll fantasy . . .

I saw fame and celebrity and its excesses take out a lot of good people who were great players and singers. They went kinda' crazy 'cause they had the means to do it and the enablers around them to help make bad things happen.

. . . Then you got the *vultures:* the handlers, agents and managers who feed the artist's ego then suck out all their money as part of the spoils of doing business. Lots of fortunes are made and lost that way.

I went through a phase briefly when I got really consumed with getting my fair share of everything, but I figured out that I wasn't sharing my music for that purpose-I just wanted to be heard; to play out to a live audience. Let my music be heard . . . making a living would follow that.

Many who knew me would joke about my single-minded purpose. I knew at some point I wasn't going to live to be an old man, much less live forever. My days had numbers on them. I had to squeeze out as much as I could from life with the time I had allotted to me.

Your soul has a timetable and the earlier you learn to budget and allocate your time in the right way-the better it flows for you-right up to the end.

My timeline was destined to be quite short, but I crammed as much into it as I could. My goal was not to be the greatest guitar player that ever lived; it was to be the best guitar player I could be; doing my music, my way, the way I heard it in my head 24/7; within that criteria, it was a success . . .

Maybe you'd like me to describe what it's like here. Of course, there are sounds, like I said before, but there are also lots of various colors . . . LOTS of colors in fantastic designs and patterns . . . Lots of people here still think of and see themselves as they were in their body life. I think of it as kind of a form of denial in a way. It means they haven't released "the surly bonds of earth" when that's their mindset; it's hard to move forward in that state.

Lots of visiting and networking goes on all the time. New arrivals are greeted and shown around. Special people are chosen as guides-a few volunteer-but mostly they are hand picked and trained to usher in new souls and help with their re-orientation. It's a good gig—you see like so many new people and they stay friends with you lots of times. Those from specific 'pods' tend to hang together . . . Sometimes people who have common interests will stay together and have long conversations about their common passion. It's all done with thoughts and pictures . . . no words.

Jesus, Holy Spirit, Jehoshiva and Eloah and other Elohim members mix in and mingle frequently and are always available to 'talk'.

Some people stay engaged protecting and looking after loved ones left behind. [Yes, they really do that] Depending on their energy level and intensity, they can affect outcomes-even if it's only a word of warning about a potential hazard.

Appearance-wise, I'd have to say we all look kinda' like the actors in the film *"Cocoon"* after they removed their flesh suits. It's a warm, glowing light energy. We're all the same in looks, rank, agenda-all are equal. There's no prejudice or jealousy-we are free to pursue all sorts of pastimes.

As a parting thought, I want to tell everyone something important that may be contrary to what you've been taught: **God does NOT judge anyone**. It is completely opposed to the way things work in the etheric world. The 3 new laws are what you need to go by because of Love, not because you're afraid of what will happen to you if you don't.

I never really thought of myself as being a teacher, but I hope my sharing some thoughts with you gave you some new things to think about and some new insights into what comes after and how it works. Thanks a lot for the opportunity.

Later,
Jimi

CHAPTER 2

John Lennon

John Lennon

"*. . . they say it's my birthday . . .*" Hello, my name is John Lennon. Today I would have been 70. God, that sounds so old when I say it . . . but I suppose not when one is living it.

There's so much I'd like to say as my contribution to this project; It's hard to know where I should start . . .

My participation in this came from a meeting I had with a cool guy I met here named Dusty. He had not been here very long and he came looking for me. Eloah introduced us and said we'd have a lot to talk about . . . and as always she was exactly right.

You might think that when people are here and they get together to talk it might be like "Where you from?" or "What are you in for?"—sorry, a joke—. Really it's all quite different than you might expect . . . or I anticipated.

Dusty said he liked my music very much-especially *Imagine*-said it always touched him in a deep way each time he heard it. I appreciated him telling me that. We spoke of our lives, our children-mostly, people we admired, those we loved, things we were involved in. He talked about his church group (Divine Way of Life Center) and The Way. I told him many things that were very personal that I would not normally tell anyone, but there was this ease between us that made it easy to trust and truly share on a deep level. I quite liked our visits.

He asked me if I remembered being shot. My answer was 'no'. I recall pain-hot, searing, blinding pain-that took my breath away and I clearly remember seeing Yoko's face and her expression, but

I couldn't tell if it was in real time or from inside my head. I was conscious of sirens, angry, urgent voices that blurred together then faded into background noise . . . then I only heard my heartbeat. I felt panic for a split second, then a calm that settled over me like a heavy fog or mist and I didn't hear my heart beating any longer-and I knew I was headed to the next 'what-ever'.

People might be interested to know if I have bad feelings toward the bloke that put all this in motion: am I angry or do I hate him or so on . . . ? The short of it is 'no'. Yes, by his actions (Chapman), I was snatched out of the lives of those I loved most dearly and my own life that was in quite a good place. It had to happen because it was time for it to happen-due to arrangements and the agreement made in the Before Days as they are known here. Of course, I didn't know at the time, not in my aware mind-my conscious mind, but my unconscious knew there was a timeline that had to be followed. Chapman did the job as it was written in the *cosmic script*.

Chapman had a whole head full of obvious reasons he thought was driving all his actions, but they were not the true motivation. I hope people can get hold of this idea.

When I got here, at first I couldn't seem to get me bearings-like being in the bloody Bermuda Triangle or something; me compass was spinning. My Mum, Mike Douglas, Brian Epstein were the first familiar faces I saw that I recognized. I had a guide holding my arm, moving me where I needed to go for different checkpoint-like stops.

One of my first clear thoughts I recall being aware of was: "All that spiritual rubbish I didn't take very seriously for so long is staring me in the face"—that's my thought. I remember thinking: 'this is all such a bad dream or a flashback or the like' . . .

Lots of people acknowledged my arrival with a smile, a nod or greeting-which was unexpected and I was a bit unsure as to how I was expected to react or respond. Of course, I knew soon that there was NO expectation to speak of . . . just guidance and direction to help me reintegrate.

Due to the suddenness of my situation, I am told some of my soul circuits experienced a kind of short circuit and needed to be 're-booted' to use a computer term. Not sure how much time elapsed before I was fully in the moment and engaged in my new surroundings. It felt odd and wonderful.

It's tough to gauge time sequences as time is not a main factor of existence here. Timing is, but not time—the concept. No reason for it really.

The first member of "Upper Management" I met was Jesus. I recognized him immediately before a word was spoken. We had an entire conversation in half a second with no words being spoken. He had this kindness vibe all about Him and emanating from Him and it was powerful-even from a distance.

Before He spoke to me I knew for certain He loved me and all was well. I started to say something about the statement that I made that was taken completely out of context; you know, about the Beatles being more popular than Jesus? It felt like an eternity since the incident, but I suddenly felt the pressing need to explain it. I didn't want Him to think I had been disrespectful as the press tried to spin it. I tried to think of how to approach the topic and what to say-should I be funny or flip . . . or be straight to the point?

Before I had a strategy, He extended His hand to me and said "Welcome John-let me introduce you to some interesting people and show you around." I took His hand and my inner self lit up like a Manhattan skyline from the power surge I felt. It was a rush of pure Love wrapped in bands of colors with vibrations around and through it. I knew instantly He understood and we never spoke of it.

One of those introductions was to Dusty and his friend, Roan.

Since I arrived, I was focused-to a point of obsession some would say-about contacting certain people I left behind to come here; Yoko, Sean and Julian, of course, and a few close friends. Dusty was the one who explained that dreams might be a good place to start that process-if I wanted to begin there. That was my initial effort to reach those I love so much.

17

Mostly, I watched what has transpired over the years-letting the situations and events seek their own levels. It was so pleasing to me that Julian and Sean both found a musical voice and pursued it. Julian is now exhibiting his photography at galleries all over. Sean will follow many pursuits as he is so inspired. It's so good that there is some peace amid my survivors. I think that time passing really does dull pain and soften memories and it amplifies the positive parts of relationships. Time essentially stopped for me on that December night, but it worked its unique magic on so many situations from my life. I am so grateful for this outcome. I am so proud of those who decided to let Love and Forgiveness be part of my legacy.

I wrote some songs, stated some obvious and not-so-obvious truths, did some beneficial things for charities and individuals, but my true legacy is two young men who are good people with good minds and good hearts. Their mums get much of the credit for that, but I know I had some influence too. It pleases me so much that my sons are friends as well as brothers.

Yoko has been extraordinary in her efforts to keep my dreams and music alive. For these things and 10,000 other things I thank her and love her.

My take on the spiritual path was altered with my association with Maharishi Mahesh Yogi. He got me to see the value of meditating and finding the quiet center within. My inner realms had been angry and ready to pop off at any moment prior to that time.

George (Harrison) was tuned in to the spiritual scene long before I was and he carried on his exploring, learning and discovery all his life. We used to chide his interest and deep desire and quest to understand his life, his destiny, God, his role to serve God, how things truly work and so on. He had a deep understanding of it all—much more than I ever did. He got the rest of us to experience what we could by awakening to our spiritual path, etc. He is near most of the time and we talk often.

He instilled in his son Dhani, his knowledge of spiritual matters. I think it will empower him to go beyond where we did with our *'dog and pony'* show.

My boys each had to seek out the proper path for themselves. Don't know for sure if that made them stronger or slowed down their awakening. Their early years were so very different because I was so different . . . the surrounding circumstances so very different. I did the best I could with what I knew at the time. Guess they'll have to tell me all about it one day.

Lots of folks I know are here and we have had a chance to reconnect like old times—only no self-medicating this time. Some wanted to come back and try it all again-some said no more volunteering for them; they prefer behind the scenes.

My music helped me figure out my life, my pain, my relationships and where I fit in the world. For a long time I didn't know where I would fit-or if I ever could or would. I owe music a big debt of gratitude. It was my therapy and it has been a huge help during my re-integration process here.

When I played onstage, all those kids screaming . . . seemed like they were trying to shout us down, not hear us or listen to our songs. We really just wanted to be heard, have fun, get girls and make money for our trouble in the beginning. When we had something to say, and a stage on which to say it, it was impossible to express it onstage. People heard our music in their cars on the radio, in their homes listening to our records and seeing us on tv shows; that's why we stopped touring and went to the studio and off the road.

The Beatles, as the world has come to know the concept, lasted a short 3 years and even now the music lives on 40 years later and counting. It was one of those 'magical moments' Jimi Hendrix spoke of earlier in this book: all the components came together exactly in Divine Time and Space and the rest is history.

When I review my life, I marvel at the journey: it was mostly a roller coaster ride, but I'm so thankful to have had the opportunity to have taken the ride with some truly great friends who happened to be great people too. There were many rewards, but there was a cost too.

My association with Paul (McCartney) was like being brothers with different mothers-with all that brings to the party: ups and downs, spats and fighting, fun and craziness and lots of laughter. We started as friends and ended as friends-the story is in the time in between. We lived it, we sang about it and we changed the world in some ways we may never know or understand. It was never our goal when it all began for the four of us, but look at the heights and depths we experienced all along the way. There were sacrifices made and the price had to be paid, karma to be worked out, messages of peace and love to be put in the public consciousness. We did all that to the best of our ability; understanding it all had to come later.

Thank God it has.

Remember: where's there's life, there's hope . . .

"Come together right now, over me"

JOHN

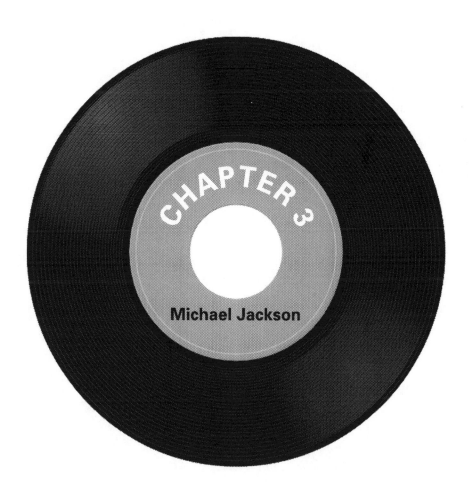

CHAPTER 3

Michael Jackson

Michael Jackson

My name is Michael Jackson. I truly welcome the opportunity to be a part of this project. I've been extremely busy since I arrived here-with my own activities, but also helping my family members-especially my Mother and my children. It's been very painful to watch everyone make the adjustments to my no longer being there; that's the ironic twist: I'm there most of the time all around them! I can no longer dry the tears of my children, but I do stroke their hair, kiss them goodnight and comfort them as best I can . . . and sing to them. There are many dear friends I left behind-true friends with great hearts and big capacities to love. I am certain of their love for me. Topping the list would be my family, (Paris, Prince and Blanket are in a separate category completely and my amazing and talented friends).

I was not prepared to make this transition-emotionally speaking. There was more I wanted to do and say and projects to complete and children to help. In many ways, it was good that I went first; having to say good-bye to my Mother and family would have been heartbreaking. The series of events did not make me think I was spending my final hours on Earth in my 'Michael' body.

My old drive was back and the future with the possibilities it held, were exciting to me again. I had been seriously considering getting back into acting in films.

All the ugly, horrible accusations, allegations and mean-spirited gossiping hurt me so deeply; I may have beat the legal charges, but there were serious scars left in the wake of it all. I was enjoying being immersed in planning, rehearsing and preparing for the tour.

I've met so many beautiful new friends here-especially the artists and performers. An interesting guy came up and introduced himself to me soon after I arrived. He said his name was Dusty and maybe he could be of some help to me as I went through the re-orientation period when I first got here. I had seen many familiar faces-but Dusty had a very kind face and demeanor, his voice was gentle and soothing and he had this amazing radiance about him. We visited often and I was introduced to his friends, but he always came alone to sit and visit. We talked about so many things . . . ! He knew so much about how this place operates and what to expect and so forth. He told me about his family, daughter and grandbaby . . . and his little church group—Divine Way of Life. He said he had arrived a short time before I did. He said my presence would be especially welcomed by two members there: Gus and Deborah. Little by little, I attempted to make contact and connections with them. Dusty suggested I might try dreams first, as a way to introduce myself to their Higher Selves. It all felt right and comfortable and now I can speak freely and they hear and sense when I am nearby. When they know it's me, they both giggle-it's very sweet.

There's a very interesting panel of consultants working on the Divine Way of Life projects. When some of the key players here heard about it, they wanted to be a part of it. They all respect and love Eloah and know how she focuses on her projects. Some of the behind-the-scenes people will contribute to this little interview project . . .

It was thought that this project would take interviews and backstage passes to another level and people who knew us or admired our work might enjoy our take on what this experience is like.

First, you should know that whatever you expect this place to look and feel like-it probably will at first. Dusty talked about teaching his students about creating a meditation place and that it will be your destination when you pass over; what a perfect concept . . . ! Wish I had been taught about that concept . . . !

I didn't really expect to see streets of gold and mansions everywhere—that's too Hollywood—even for me, I guess, but everything was visually very different from what my fantasy had been since childhood.

Initially, upon arriving here, all your senses feel like they are at their utmost breaking point: everything is red-lined, maxed out; then things begin to wind down a little at a time. It started to feel more comfortable to me. Other musicians I've spoken to said they felt this same 'overload' sensation, but others did not.

Next, I noticed the atmosphere was beautiful and the temperature was perfect. One thing I really liked was people I knew greeted me, but it was low key-nobody made a big fuss. Welcoming and warm greeting-I felt like people were glad I was here with them.

Once I cleared my senses and started to look around, I was shocked by how good everything smelled . . . and the 'vibe' of the place. Everyone called me "Michael" not Mr. Jackson. The air was thick with the "Love Vibe" everywhere I went . . . everyone I met or saw.

Things are interesting colors-often unexpected and extremely aesthetically pleasing to the eye-just not what I was used to seeing.

Grass was blue and the sky was green-both pleasing shades-just different from my Earth plane experience. It soon becomes clear that you are "through the looking glass".

If you can stay in the moment, changing how you think about things is much easier. Things just are what they are. I am assured that this was also true in the Earth plane, but it's so easy to become distracted . . .

. . . Then there's the layer upon layer of the most exquisite celestial sounds, tones and music. I was quickly engulfed by it and its multiple layers. If you can think of it as scoring a chart for an orchestra and how the parts are layers for harmonies, sub-tones and harmonies-that's the closest I can get to attempting to explain it. Nearly all are smiling and glad to be here-shed of their 'cloak' of a human body.

All you music lovers-here's an insider tip: the creative process is alive and well and fully functional. It's much easier to be creative here than in your world and people are always asking me to partner up to write, jam or play a new song project.

9-24-10 (Michael continues)

The flow of creativity is as evident as air to breathe and the cool part is not only is it allowed, but encouraged and it's received without judgment-only appreciation . . . that's some people's concept of heaven . . .

As I have the opportunity, I want to say some things I need to say: destiny and hard work, talent and awareness, love and truth; all parts of The Way-especially the unconditional love portion. The depth of my caring, compassion and efforts to show love were often misinterpreted, misunderstood and ultimately misjudged. God knew and continues to know the content of my heart and the essence of my intent. If I were the monster the media and my accusers portrayed me to be, I can say with certainty, I would not have been allowed to be a contributor to this project.

The allegations hurt me on a soul level. I knew the truth and had to hold fast to it. I came to understand that those pointing the accusatory fingers really didn't matter. The matter at hand was between God and me and was all along. Upon my arrival here and subsequent visits I have had with Eloah and others, I feel redeemed, accepted and loved beyond measure.

The status of children in the world community should be elevated in my view. Their safety, health, education, care and upbringing should be a world priority-not an afterthought. They are vulnerable, trusting, loving and innocent until adults destroy or spoil those traits. They should not be regarded as "disposable", placed in dumpsters and the front porches of strangers. Of all that God has made, children are in the top 3 . . . they should be regarded as precious treasures on loan to us by God.

Eloah told me that when a young child prays, it is given the highest priority and the entities give each prayer and child the utmost attention possible. That's impressive! If adults would follow the example and love God and interact with Them as children do, the relationship would be much improved.

Families matter. The adage that you choose your friends but inherit your family is just blatantly <u>wrong</u>. The fact is you <u>do</u> choose your parents, siblings and all the clan. It's all put together by a consensus agreement in the *Before Time* prior to launching back into the next incarnation. **There is NO perfection to be found in families**. If you are looking for that, you are destined for disappointment. They can be extremely valuable for lots of different reasons:

a. They can be the bedrock upon which the foundation of your life is built;
b. They teach you values-often by observations of what NOT to do;
c. They teach you humor, laughter, tears and love-what it is and what it is not.

Families are like a little microcosm of the world-where you can work on your "chops" and rehearse the variety of person you want to be. The thing to keep in mind is this: you teach as much as you learn. **Everyone is a student as well as a teacher in every interaction you have.**

I gave my family everything I had. When I had my three children, my complete focus was on them and I spent every minute I could with them. I'm so glad I made the choice to do that. I feel I provided a good foundation for them. Outsiders perceived it as bizarre or unorthodox, but they could not know what was appropriate in our circumstances.

Much attention was focused on the unusual bits of my life, but I can tell you my life was a complete blessing; start to finish, entrance to exit and all in between . . . it didn't seem so at the time, but I've had time to put everything into perspective.

The last thing on the list is to introduce your children to God as a best friend upon whom they can always depend. Don't do them the disservice of thinking 'damn' is God's last name instead of **LOVE**. That gift is singularly the most loving gift or legacy a parent or grandparent can create for the children in their life. Avoid teaching them that God lives in a big house with a pointy roof, but rather in all things around us. The etheric world where all the best things happen is neither above nor below: it is all around and through everything.

I have asked to be a special consultant on the Divine Way of Life projects of Dusty's merry little band of friends and followers. It would be my pleasure and honor to assist in Eloah's work. There may not be any glitter gloves or moon-walking, but you might see an imprint to know Michael had his hand in it. I love you all!

MJ

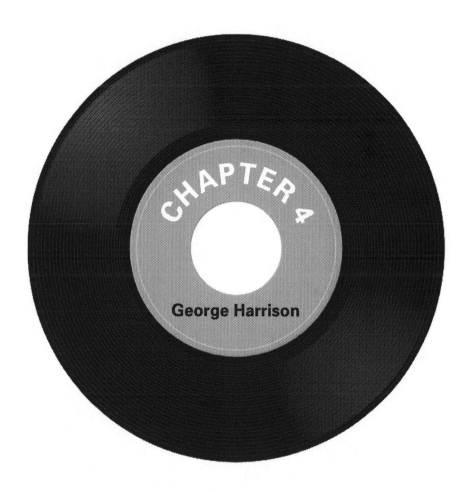

CHAPTER 4

George Harrison

George Harrison

Hello everyone-my name is George Harrison; so glad it's finally my turn to speak . . . I used to be a member of a quartet that got some airplay on both sides of the Atlantic back in the 60's. I played lead guitar and wrote some tunes and sang a bit. When the four were no more, I struck out on my own and played with friends, dabbled at making films and produced some records for several artists.

As a boy growing up in Liverpool, I have to say I was very ordinary in most ways . . . I was quite shy. With several females in the house, it was a bit difficult to get a word in sideways at times, so I listened more than I spoke.

This "observer role" made me appear '*mysterious*' and '*complex*' . . . which was fine 'cause the girls seemed to find it appealing-even from middle school through several serious relationships into me 20's. I was called "*the quiet one*" by the press and fan mags.

As I grew into my teens, I found that my guitar could speak for me and I was much more comfortable playing than conversing with people I didn't know. I decided at quite a young age to really learn the techniques to play guitar well-at least well enough to play and make some money. At that time, most jobs a bloke my age might get, paid very little: grocery stores or sweeping or helping deliver things for stores-I wanted more.

I did the school bit as long as I could. It was a good place to meet friends-both boys and girls. I always liked reading and my curiosity about lots of things led me to read many books on whatever my passion of the week might be.

The learning maze I made for myself is what led me to explore spirituality and religion. In the 1960's, the *Mods* and *Rockers* were setting all the fashion trends and influencing art and especially the music scene around the London area; that whole scene gained momentum and soon it was seen all over the urban areas of England-from all directions it fanned out.

In retrospect, it was a bit like gang mentality-you know, **US vs. THEM.** Newspaper and magazine writers had to label things that they wrote about-or so they thought. The Beatles were regarded as a *'Mod'*' thing; the Rolling Stones more *'Rockers'*-all based mostly on appearance and off-stage behavior: who we dated, drank with, played with, had our pictures taken with-that was the scene. It lasted for awhile, but as all trends do, it evolved into the next thing.

It was during this phase of English young society that musicians considered part of the *'Mods'*—which included most of the Mersey beat bands-were often seen out with models (also a big part of that lifestyle). Musicians and models: an attraction that still draws talented people together even today. I was attracted to and was introduced to several models. The one that shined the brightest to me was Patti Boyd-a beautiful girl and popular trend-setter and trend-maker in hip English culture. We got together and stayed together for awhile.

As the progression was happening from the *Mod/Rocker* scene to *Carnaby Street*, etc., inner changes were happening-not just exterior changes or appearances. Young people were looking deeper into themselves and each other. By the time *The Quarrymen* had evolved into the *Fab Four,* we found ourselves in the midst of the whirlwind-like the eye of a hurricane.

People we met (and there were a LOT of people we met) who were always trying to turn us on to one thing or another: new artist, new band, new drug, new club . . . It was always "Man, you gotta try this" or "Let me show you what this is all about" (i.e. new author, new book, new idea and philosophy). I had many interesting conversations with new people who always seemed to be encircling us about philosophy, spirituality, different religions, ideas and practices. My path in this direction was a long and winding one to be sure. I had to pick my way carefully through all the various influences until I started feeling I had found some TRUTHS. The other guys usually referred to my quest and readings as "spiritual rubbish"—especially John.

Speaking of John, he was among the first I saw when I arrived here. We embraced and it was like no time had passed. It was he and some others who helped me with re-orientation and getting settled in here. I saw lots of people I knew early on upon getting here. They have in turn introduced me to many new friends. I was assured I could take all the time I needed to begin to feel at home again. I was really amazed at how quickly the transition was made. I was hoping maybe I could play in the dirt and start a small garden in a quiet corner somewhere. Turns out, you can do virtually anything you want to because everything is totally in the moment-which suits me fine.

I have the option and opportunity to look in on and visit Olivia and Dhani whenever I want and I exercise this option as often as I can.

Dhani has many talents and skills and watching him create a path in his life has been very gratifying and interesting. He still has his Mum to support him and to be there to share in his accomplishments and near misses too. It wouldn't be fun without those.

I'm glad my growing garden legacy is in place at Briar Park. I had many hours of peaceful puttering and planting in the dirt there. I always felt in a good place with my hands in the soil on my knees. It was spiritual really . . .

Another friend I see often is Linda McCartney . . . a great lady here as she was on the earth plane. We had many things in common we could speak about: our illnesses, our families, the 'glory days'- what a whirlwind it was for us all. She keeps busy helping out her family when they need her. Her transition left gaps in Paul and the children's lives, but Linda had been a 'hands-on' Mum and her clan had a solid foundation to build on so everyone is doing interesting and creative work. Paul was very lucky to have had so many years with his great love . . . what a head and heart full of memories he has . . . ! They are still strongly connected.

Lots of conversations here . . . all the time-about every topic imaginable. The Elohim are often engaged in these talks. As usual, I like to listen-I learn so much from each session.

Listening is an art. Most people are more fond of talking and strive to be a good speaker. I came to realize and understand that by mastering the art of listening, it feeds all your other activities. In my case, it helped me with my music (to be sure); to understand the essence of people (the obvious and unobvious); and to find my way to God. That journey was a long one with many detours, but as all the spiritual leaders are fond of saying, "it's not how you start, but how you end that counts". I have a sense of peace in knowing I achieved that life goal I set for myself. I spent time teaching and talking to Dhani about it too. I hope his journey to God will be smoother than mine had to be. At least he knew at a young age that there was a path to God, but he would have to find it in his own time and way.

I had many years to work out soul issues as I became aware of them. Meditation was a primary tool in achieving this awareness. Anyone reading this . . . I would urge and encourage you to use meditation as your stepping stone towards achieving the knowledge, understanding and wisdom and friendship with God-whatever name you attach to that entity. **Prayer** is important too, but that is you talking to God; **Meditation** is when you are quiet so God can speak to you. Simply profound, isn't it?

Building relationship with one's guides, angels, higher self and Divine Family is certainly worth the time and effort it takes to do so. The kindness, humor, wisdom, compassion and especially the LOVE to be gotten is too immense to describe here. Once you get back here, you recognize all those entities with whom you had spent so much time. It makes transition so much easier when you know you'll be welcomed by friends in high places.

The Eastern spirituality taught me about reincarnation and meditation and a thousand other insightful things. Western beliefs are good up to a point, but it's like hitting a glass ceiling because they disallow so much as even being possible. If they can't support it in conventional scripture interpretation, they say it's "of the devil" and all conversation ceases, which means ideas and possibilities stopped being exchanged.

By world culture standards, America is a relatively new culture, and as such, they have the attitude many young people do: I call it "ideological arrogance". It goes something like this: "This is our belief, it's been our belief from the beginning and to change it would be falling into the devil's plan". It's impossible to converse with folks who hold this belief.

Islam beliefs are structured the same, only the extremist factions go after the offending speaker to do bodily harm. It's their belief and NO others need apply. I believe that's why they've been consistently at war somewhere in the world-all the time-for 6000 years.

Love cannot prevail when civility and respect for others cannot exist.

The teachings of the Way and staying true to the center path allows for discussion with others of differing opinions and belief systems. It is based on Divine Love and is unconditional in nature.

Jesus taught the principles of the Way and now it will soon be available to the world . . . very soon.

In the Earth plane there are so many options to pursue to find one's way to God. People sometimes get so overwhelmed they give up without having achieved the goal. To be a seeker is to never take the path of least resistance. It is usually a long, arduous process where the only rewards are inner knowing and satisfaction.

Always remember this wise directive: **The best path to God is the best way you can get there . . . and it's different for every single person on the planet. Get there the best way you can.**

I think it would be amazing if all our sons could get together and play-maybe just collaborate and record, not tour . . . **RISING SONS** featuring Zak, Dhani, Sean, Julian, James . . . just a thought . . .

[Perhaps I should describe my experiences here-you might like to compare mine with the other contributors]

The first thing I felt was to be free of an ailing physical form-like taking off a very heavy suit of armor. A-a-h-hhhh what a relief that was! No pain, drug regimen schedule . . . all gone. I was Light . . . literally! I noticed that immediately as I travelled to this place of souls.

Next was the speed at which things happened: blinding speed, speed of thought I recall thinking.

Being greeted by familiar folks was the next step. Getting your bearings and getting settled in.

There are brilliant hues of color everywhere and the flow of creative energy never stops or slows down. The energy is palpable here and in every form you can imagine. Creative people here are reveling and creating in it all the time. Must be the closest thing to the concept of heaven maybe? Could be!

[break]

Sun. 10-24-10

I suppose I should state that this channeling project is a completely new experience for me . . . to communicate through someone as I am now working with and through Deborah. I haven't attempted to do so in any way or anyone 'til now. I feel a bit unsteady and like trying to do anything for the first go round, a bit shaky 'til I get me rhythm going so to speak.

There's so much I could say about my life on the earth plane-childhood, school days, finding my way to music and all it brought into my life, my family, health, legal issues, being attacked, losing friends [and there were so many over the years] . . . I'm not sure what someone reading this would really want to know. It's odd isn't it? The quiet Beatle gets the global stage to say anything he pleases and he doesn't know where to begin . . . !

First, Eloah is telling-encouraging actually-me to address finding my voice. My musical experience gave me an inner confidence to express myself and I wrote quite a bit of music-in terms of volumes of material.

Since John and Paul wrote so many songs, sometimes I had a hard time getting mine to be included. I now see that situation was another step in finding my voice: speaking up during recording sessions and making the case as to why a particular song should be added to the line up on an album project. The "White Album" allowed me to put more of my material out to the fans . . . and critics.

My songs covered a broad spectrum of genres: spiritual topics and sitar music to top 10 radio play. Going through the tunes and choosing the ones to include nearly always caused a row to some extent. Sometimes, certain members stopped speaking to other members; made for a very difficult environment in which to be a contributor. For some projects I just showed up, put my tracks down on tape as needed then I'd leave. Ringo would sometimes stay around the studio more than I did. The boys would explain and show me the song and my bit in it. I would provide the part and that would be it.

The tension was so thick much of the time, I didn't know if some albums would ever get finished so they could be released. The Apple label really needed to keep the revenues flowing, so sometimes money truly had the last word.

It was always ironic to me that our favorite thing as a band was to play to an audience. In the early years it was actually paid rehearsal to work out new songs to put into the song list rotation, but we had to travel and gig as much as possible to earn a living. When we became the Fab Four, playing and touring became impossible. Nobody came to hear us play, they came to scream and have a

'Beatle experience'. We could have left all the gear unplugged and gone through the motions and no one would have noticed. We gained creative freedom and control that being in your own studio can afford you, but it took awhile to get accustomed to the new lifestyle.

When I think of how much time we all spent together-traveling, recording, hotels, etc.-it was a huge amount of time: certainly to really be like brothers on different levels. We sort of filled in the "family gaps" some of us had felt since we were very young boys.

When Paul said he wanted out and the ripple effect hit everyone else, it was a chaotic emotional time.

The split had a favorable side for the fans. Instead of a band called the Beatles making music, there were four musicians *formerly known as Beatles* producing music. The individual projects were so different. Paul and Linda had *Wings* plus he collaborated with several artists in the 80's. John and Yoko had their band plus art projects. Ringo recorded and toured and got into more film work. I had my collaborations, solo recordings and concerts plus I produced some new artists and developed some film projects.

Sometimes we all talked, sometimes some of us didn't.

The energy that was created by the 4 of us had such a far reaching effect-as to be historical in today's consciousness. There are college courses on our music, books, films, photos, TV retrospectives, etc . . . and it still rolls forward even today—nearly 40 years later. How could 4 young blokes from obscure blue collar backgrounds have ever predicted such events? Short answer: ***nobody did***!

To everyone's credit, all have used the wealth energy that was created to support some great causes in big ways-bringing them to the attention of the public. The 'giving back' I feel has been the factor that regulated any karma that was created. The other factor was we started saying useful things about love-Universal love. "All You Need Is Love" was the first global link video feed of its kind to ever be done. It was the message: Eloah and the Divine Family wanted the message and its energy to get out on a global scale . . . and it did.

This project is at a similar point where message, history and technology (and willing participants, of course) have all met at the same juncture of space and time. The social networking that is so available now will make getting the message of Unconditional Love-the essence of the Way and its teachings-instantly available to the people of the world. No one has to hike into the Himalayas to study with the Masters of Enlightenment. They are bringing the message to the masses through personal electronic devices-though only a small percentage will be actively looking for it.

I would urge people reading my words here to use technology to get your soul's questions answered. Here are some ideas to think about:

1. *Learn to meditate . . . the correct way*
2. *Become acquainted with the Divine Family essence*
3. *Make it a point to be loving and kind*
4. *Put into practice things you learn*
5. *Learn the 7 Universal Laws and practice their lessons*
6. *Learn to forgive-it opens huge doors of opportunities for you. It's truly a gift you give yourself.*
7. *KNOW YOU ARE LOVED-ALL THE TIME*
8. *You have more than 1 life to get it right . . . Relax!*
9. *Give peace a chance*

I have read many books, listened to many teachers and travelled to many destinations to learn what I just listed. I could have learned them at home on the Internet-had it existed in those days. Many of us used drugs to attempt to open the doors to our unconscious-and to quiet the clattering din in our conscious mind. I saw it was hindering my search for self-realization, so I stopped.

Trust me: meditation is a better choice.

Understand please, that God is "All that is" and simply stated, it boils down to Love of the highest magnitude and purest form in existence. Invite it to be in your life, be friends with Them without fear. If you follow my advise while you are 'there' (in the Earth plane) . . . you won't have to digest it all once you get 'here' (etheric plane).

I appreciate Eloah making this opportunity available to me. I hope my insights will be found to be of help to someone who might be seeking some truthful answers to persistent questions that won't be quiet in their minds.

I thank Deborah (for her dictation and many other skills) and her partner Gus for the work they are doing together to get this information out on a global level.

Maybe there will be more projects like this in the future. If so, I would welcome the opportunity to speak again.

My parting thought is "Love is all you need" and the fundamental teachings of the Way will take you where you always wanted to be- back to God . . . whatever name you may use for the Power greater than yourself. The journey is not easy, but believe me when I say it's worth taking the trip.

Ji ceta rom: from the god within me to the god within you

George Harrison

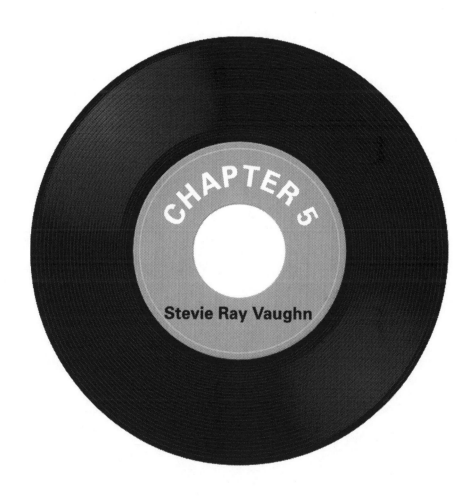

CHAPTER 5

Stevie Ray Vaughn

Stevie Ray Vaughn

Texas Tornado

Hey everybody! It's Stevie Ray Vaughn ready to talk now. I've had things to say for a long time, but I wasn't ready 'cause I didn't have all the information together. I'm ready to talk now and Eloah has been her usual kind and benevolent self and invited me to be a part of this project.

Instead of <u>For the Record</u> as the working title for this collection of recollections, I thought using the title of one of my songs "*TIC-TOC*" would fit very well . . . and you have my permission to use it. ". . . Tic-toc, tic-toc . . . time's ticking away . . ."

Relatively speaking, I've been here a pretty long period of time. By standards here, it's been about a minute and a half; by Earth plane time-more than a decade . . . seems like I just blinked my eyes and switched locations.

Since this project is focused on input from the "musically inclined", I must repeat what others have said before me: the collection of talented individuals cannot be successfully described. Everywhere I look is someone I played with, listened to, watched their show, learned from—it's a mega network!

When I understood how the classical masters were coming back as rock players and the classical listeners were being so snooty and judgmental about the genre' of music-that it was somehow 'less than music', certainly less than classical—I laughed my ass off!

The keyboard player, guitarist, or drummer were the same cats the "aficionados' had statues of sitting in their library and on their grand piano at home. Maybe it's just me, but I think the irony of that is funny as hell . . . anybody else think so?

The classical artists didn't stay here long between Earth visits. They wanted to go back ASAP. I think they dig all the electronic capabilities they can create with and how they can control the frequencies, vibrations, harmonics and have control of an entire orchestra that's stored in the memory of a computer-complete with sound sampling. Mozart, Bach, Beethoven, Handel, Chopin-so many others . . . they were kids in a candy store once they got their hands on the new technology instruments and immediately saw the potential-LIMITLESS POTENTIAL-I must say.

Some of the residents here really prefer this environment and just hang out here. Sometimes, if the chemistry and vibe is a good match, the Elohim suggests someone who is willing to channel and allow us to play through them. Usually they are young kids or guys who play in their garage or basement. Sometimes . . . they can utilize a performing artist who's in front of a live crowd; of course the energy is completely different, but both ways are too much fun to pass up. There are few things that feel as good in a player's hand as a fretboard on the neck of a guitar.

Some of the others have spoken about jamming and writing and collaborating here. Oh yeah . . . goes on all the time; Wish we had "dimension—pod" so y'all could check it out! They'd have to create a new category at the Grammy's for what's done here!

The band of energy that circles the planet that contains the new thought energy and the new music of the cosmos and the spheres is at our fingertips here.-we practically breathe it into ourselves with every breath, it rubs off of bushes and plants as we walk past—(figuratively speaking). It's like walking outside on a sunny day and feeling the sun's rays and warmth on you at all times-you're just bathed in it!

Those who have a particular skill-like music or science or writing or painting-just create like mad all the time if they choose to: hell, they don't get tired or have to eat . . . makes more time to get busy doing what lights up your soul!

The Elohim and their associates greet you and get you settled in once you arrive; then you get to choose every day what you want to do and with whom. I can sit and jam all day with Brother Ray Charles or listen to Abe Lincoln or Mark Twain tell funny stories. My only job is to decide what I want to do today.

It's not selfish or self-centered to be in that place. It is what it is, man. Freedom of choice, free will . . . you are the designer and architect of your existence. You lose track of that to some extent while you're doing your thing in the Earth plane-plus so many damn distractions that help you lose sight of your purpose . . . That there is one slippery-ass slope as we say in Texas . . . !

Here, everyone is who they were created to be: no modifications required, no judgment, no critics. You are free to be yourself in all your splendor and glory-whatever that looks like, or in some cases, sounds like.

I miss those that I shared a love connection with: my wife, my brother, my partner, my band, my friends and fans. I have visited them when it was possible to do so. Sometimes I slide into a dream or hang out on the tour bus for a little while. I missed playing in clubs and big concert venues for awhile, but that faded right away. I missed the music scenes in different cities like Austin, LA, New York, Atlanta, Tokyo, London-each place had like a pulse that reflected the heart of the people in that area . . . and it never lied-EVER! If you could read or feel the vibe and wrap your music about and through it-it was instant connection to the audience.

When I was drinking so much, I dulled out some things and amplified others almost to where I couldn't bear it. Physical senses got sharper. Guess it was like auto-pilot! I always marveled at how people could still play, when they could scarcely stand up . . . auto-pilot!

Back to the energy band for a sec . . . it's there for everybody to tap into. All it takes is desire and awareness. The knowledge, ideas, and information that's contained in that thing is limitless and is constantly fed and refreshed **all the time**-not just from our spheres, but elsewhere too. Remember I said "COSMOS . . . and it's the God's truth."

I wanted to be a contributor on this project for several reasons:

First, when my chopper went down and it was lights out for the kid, I was kinda' flitting around trying to get my bearings and I saw a point of light and focused on it. Turns out, it was Deborah, ironing and watching a cowboy movie on a Sunday afternoon in Humble, Texas.

We never met, don't think she even knew my name, but we were able to connect at that time. I kept leaning on her inner 'door bell' 'til she answered. I explained what dying looked like, felt like, and sounded like. I had to communicate by writing through her at that time as she was in her early stages of developing her spiritual talents, gifts, and skills as were we all. I really appreciated what she did for me-even though she chickened out of delivering a message to my partner. Maybe he'll read this and know I always think of him and the others. . . . So that's how I knew I could trust my thoughts to be expressed accurately here.

There's so much misinformation being put out to the public-it's conflicting or erroneous or jaded or just plain fiction! I thought I can present the truth and maybe people will have less fear or no fear of what comes after.

PEOPLE: I gotta get this one key thing across to you-God's Truth: What you do and experience in the Earth plane is like a hologram:

Your thoughts made manifest=your life experiences.

They seem real, they feel like that's all there is. Hell, I thought so too, 'til I got back here and started to remember the true order of things! The Earth experience-generally speaking-focuses on the information collected by the senses . . . usually thought to be 5 senses. That's true, but it stops short of being complete. There are other senses: at least **2** for most people and more for some who are more evolved. That's 2 (or more) <u>complete new sets of data</u> for the mind to process and give the unconscious to store as memory.

The process of the unconscious and how it is part of the master file called the Akashic Records is so extraordinary yet the vast majority of people have no clue about it. The Akashic Records are like the Library of Congress for all people who ever lived on Earth. All files of memory from the unconscious are downloaded and stored there forever. Every act, thought, word, deed-positive or negative—it's all there in unedited form. The files can be accessed and reviewed whenever one wants to take a look-you just gotta learn the how-to process. It's not complicated: 80% of it is understanding that it's there and you are free to review at your leisure.

Lots of valuable information can be discovered upon accessing your own personal file: Who you have been in all your previous lives, what you did, who was there, your contract details each time, karma issues . . . it's ALL there. The depth of understanding you can get from it is beyond explanation.

<u>Another valuable thing to know</u>: prejudice and bigotry is the height of stupidity, not to mention a total waste of time and energy. Why? Simple. Everyone has been every race, religion, both male and female, skinny and fat, really smart or dumb as a rock, talented in many different ways . . . so to be judging folks as 'not good as' or 'less than' or 'better than' is ridiculous! We are all drops of water in the same ocean and to hate the drop next to you or all around you serves NO purpose whatsoever.

<u>Something you might find interesting to know:</u> you hang out and interact with pretty much the same crew life after life. The dynamics change all the time, but the essential players are the same. Here's a good example: You've all seen John Wayne movies, right? Every film has mostly the same actors. They were cast in different roles, but

Dub Taylor, Ben Johnson, Dean Smith, Patrick Wayne, Red Steagall and others were in many of Mr. Wayne's movies; sometimes cast as Civil War soldiers, cowboys, World War II soldiers-but the same faces in different roles/characters and movies. Do you follow what I'm saying?

Each soul is part of a **POD**-or specific group of souls-sorta' like your "gang" or "posse". (Groups of whales are called PODS too) When someone decides to head back into the Earth plane and the scenario is put together, the same group usually volunteers or is asked to help pull it off.

The entity who was your Dad last time might be your daughter this time; your Granddad might be your sister-the roles are assigned to best achieve the desired outcome of the contract. Everyone has to be in agreement as to their parents, geographic location, lesson to be learned, death scenario . . . every key element has to be worked out and agreed to. Guess I needed to experience falling out of the sky . . . well, check that one off the list!

Seriously, each of my family members and their contributions towards shaping me through my childhood years, teenage years and young adult years-each was a stepping stone to build to a crescendo where I had to make some tough decisions about living and dying. Once I had worked out most of the kinks and all was rolling along pretty smoothly-finally; it was time to move on.

WRITE THIS DOWN: It's not about arriving, it's about planning the trip and the journey. Once you figure most of it out, you don't need to be here anymore. What is "IT"? It's Love, brother . . . no more complicated than that.

People used to ask me what music meant to me and where did it come from for me to play like I did? Most blues players would probably say it comes from your guts-and that's partially true. I knew when I was 'connected' 'cause I didn't think about anything specific—I focused on getting out of the way and letting the music come out *through* me-not *from* me. I couldn't really explain it that way when I was doing it, but that was what was going on.

I never considered myself a 'bible-banger' or religious guy. I did think and feel with a sense of certainty that there was a Higher Power that kept the order of the Universe so finely tuned. I thought of it as God, but my mental image was nothing like the reality. God was always pictured as an old dude with white hair and beard, stern expression with a lightning bolt in one hand and the other raised to strike something. All that imagery is man-made, bears no resemblance to the God you interact with in your heart, mind and soul (on the Earth plane) and the members of the Elohim you get to visit and hang with in this place.

Eloah Va Daath appears to me as a beautiful lady; very feminine with long blonde hair, extremely kind and loving, very lively in her discussions, has strong and informed opinions on all things, loves to help people connect and is always introducing people and arranging meetings and get-togethers. She is God-the feminine; Mother God. [She apparently appears and is described differently by other people.] Don't bother trying to argue around the Father-Mother God idea. Anything else is just wrong or misinformed. Remember in Creation we were created in their image-**male and female . . .** hey, I can't make this stuff up. I'm here to tell you straight.

Father God appears older than Eloah. I notice He's less outgoing in personality and most contact with Him is usually indirect because of His mega wattage energy levels. Eloah buffers hers some way so it doesn't "burn out" people around her.

There's a huge complement of angels of various sorts and purposes always on call ready to go into action at a word from Eloah or Elohim, Jesus or Jehoshiva. They have to be directed by a higher superior in rank. They are all specialists at all sorts of things and that's how they get their assignments.

The Protector Arch Angels-like Michael and Gabriel are H-U-G-E in size and very focused-not a lot of people skills. Intense-that's how I would describe them, but there is no one else I would ever want to protect me than those two. They are at least 9 or 10 feet tall by Earth standards, very muscular, attractive, handsome/rugged faces and both have very large swords in scabbards at their sides. I've only seen them a time or two. Very impressive.

Jehoshiva is the entity who will be making an appearance in the Earth plane in the very near future. I really like this guy. He's the youngest of the Elohim and few people know of him or recognize his name. Eloah has been his mentor and teacher along with many others-helping to prepare him to bring the Christ Consciousness back to Earth. Mark your Day Runners . . . Jehoshiva will be bringing the Christ Consciousness back in the Earth plane NOT Jesus. [Remember: the second coming of Christ in the scriptures . . . not Jesus] Jehoshiva is the most beautiful entity possibly ever created. He's attractive physically, very loving, extremely intelligent, hilariously funny and very wise.

Speaking of funny, Jesus and his Mother, Mary, are available much of the time. They seem to really like interacting with everybody. They are so funny, but wise at the same time. Their funny stories have poignant lessons to them. I really like sitting and hearing them talk about all kinds of topics.

In case you're wondering, there are lots of Texans from Farah Fawcett and Patrick Swayze to LBJ, Ann Richards and Sam Houston. Just so you know, Texas pride doesn't stop at the grave . . . Non-Texans get tired of the bravado, but they humor us-guess that's because there's so many of us.

Here's a tip you can use: *Don't look up when you pray or talk to God*; Look to either side or in front of you. The spiritual realm where we all live is all around you and through you. It's a dimensional thing. We live in the spaces between the molecules of your world-almost like a parallel universe. We function right along side you every day.

Earth people might call this place heaven because of the prevalent attitude of Love and atmosphere of harmony, but technically it's not what we were all taught about heaven . . . that place, as such, does not exist. Neither does hell; they are both states of mind that you carry over to soul level. You can create either for yourself; you manifest whatever you get.

Here's another one to write down-real important: *God doesn't do stuff TO you-only FOR you*; **[Write this down in ink in really big letters]** . . . and quit blaming God for all the things that suck in your world. You manifested it, not Them. Also . . . they cannot intervene without you asking them to participate; to do so would be interfering not assisting-big breaking of the rules.

GOD WORKS WITH PROBABILITIES AND PERCENTAGES; They are not puppeteers pulling all Mankind's strings. **Two words**: FREE WILL . . . makes that impossible and it's inherent to the design.

Large scale disasters are marvels of spiritual logistics. Getting like-minded souls with the same destiny in the same place at the same time for a common experience . . . NO small task. This is true for plane crashes, sinking ships, battles, natural events (hurricanes, tornados, etc.). There is a method to all this loss of life. It's not cold, calloused or heartless to say it, it's Divine Truth. If it were not so, Eloah would block me from saying it.

ANOTHER BIGGIE TO WRITE DOWN:

God Does Not Judge You. You are loved beyond comprehension and blessed beyond measure: judgment that results in the express elevator going up or down is just not how it works. NOTE: this includes lifestyle choices (i.e. gay or not) God wants you to be a good person-doesn't give a flip about your sexual preferences or orientation. 'Adam & Eve not Adam & Steve' is a man-made and mean spirited sentiment. Jesus said," Love one another as I have loved you". There was no *'p.s except gay folks'*.

YOU NEED TO KNOW THIS—PEOPLE, <u>THIS IS HUGE</u>:

Another name for the 'dark' side is *Metatron*-aka:Lucifer, Satan, Morning Star and other names. Really exists-alive and well and very active. Metatron is his true name. Started out as an arch angel of the highest rank (like Michael and Gabriel). Took unprecedented step of deciding he'd like to move up to upper management and made himself the title 'Lord God'. Lots of the Old Testament including Creation is full of Metatron activities. The Ten Commandments were his way to control people so they would be easier to manage. Jesus changed the Ten Commandments to the Three Directives:

 a. *Love God with your heart, mind & soul*
 b. *Love your neighbor as yourself*
 c. *See the beauty in all things*

That's it. Simple.

Some people around the world advertise having classes about angels and include Metatron as a angel of light: one to pray to or to invoke-big mistake: HUGE!. Disengage from anything Metatron related. He is the CEO of the Dark Side. Christians refer to him as The Enemy . . . Believe it . . . he is.

Metatron has a big recruiting push on now to gather and organize followers. His team has finally figured out a way to get to people through their electronics: cell phones, computers, tv's, videos, gps, anything electronic. It is critically important that you pray for protection of yourself morning and evening. Bless all your electronics to protect them from being used against you.

Please heed what I have written here. It is Divine Truth . . . it's serious business. I'm telling you to help you in the days to come.

Maybe you'll hear me playing out somewhere when you least expect it . . . until then . . .

Adios,
SRV

CHAPTER 6

Ray Charles

11-2-10   **Ray Charles**

Hey everybody . . . you can call me Ray if you're my friend—Mr. Charles if you're not.

What a trip to get asked to make an appearance in this collection! I told Eloah lots of people reading these pages may not even know who I am (or was)-much less care much what ol' Ray has to say from the big ol' stage in the sky.

I'll be leaving soon for another visit into the Earth plane: got all the plans made, agreements done and got it all approved-just waiting on the timing to be right. That's one reason I wanted to talk to all you good folks.

My time on Earth was a roller coaster ride—from my days as a poor youngster in the South to playing the biggest venues on the planet as a headliner. From having no shoes to playing for European royalty—Man, that's a ride!

One thing that helped me weather the ups and downs was my ability to keep my sense of humor in the worst situation all the way to the best situations. If you can still laugh in the face of adversity-*it ain't nothin' but a thang*!

People used to ask me lots of questions about my being blind. I had my stack of pat answers I used for years, but I'll tell y'all something that you might can use at some point: Not having visual capability helped me to develop the ability to communicate mentally with pictures. That skill was very useful in easing back into the old crowd here in the etheric plane. I had lots of pictures in my head from my young days-before I lost my sight. It (losing my sight) was gradual and I did have memories of many colors and images.

Music was a great equalizer for my life. I developed the skill to play, the ear to hear the parts of the harmonies, I had a sense of rhythm and I could make a good living while having a ball. I learned quick that money is color blind. Something in the timbre of my voice when I sang a blues song or a dance tune with a beat-people listening could connect to it somehow. My friend 'Q' (Quincy Jones) used to say it was the "'soul' in soul music. You can't learn it, you can't teach it, you can't fake it, you can't deny it. It's its own thing. Your music has it-lots of folks will relate to the vibe. If you don't have it, your road to a big successful career with staying power will be a rocky one for sure. Lots of guys-old and young-give up without getting their goal of success with the music they write, play or sing.

I was blessed-no other way to say it. The measure of success I enjoyed made it possible to help some great charitable and humanitarian causes. I was pleased and happy to join in events where the cause was the "star" not the people singing the songs. "We Are the World" was such a thing. The "Farm Aid "shows, Jerry Lewis MD Telethons-these are a few of the thousands of events to which I lent my name, face and voice. I feel good I could give back in such a way over the years.

There's a special reason I agreed to get in this project-kinda' personal that nobody ever knew or discussed, but I was made aware of it a short time ago. It involves the lady taking all this dictation notes from all of us: Miss Deborah.

One of the many times I appeared in Houston, Texas was at the big Houston Livestock Show and Rodeo they have every year. It's huge . . . ! I played that venue several times, but around 2000, I played it and Ronnie Milsap opened for me. The place was full of folks really digging the set Ronnie played. I came out and fronted a small jazz-type band. As is fairly common in such venues, there were sound system issues-despite a good sound check earlier in the day. My vocals weren't coming through well and the music overpowered them. People walked out during the performance and left the stadium after just a few tunes. Deborah was at the show. I didn't notice the walk-outs, but she did. She said a prayer that night that the incident would not hurt my feelings and affect my opinion of Houston people in a bad way. She worried my feelings would be hurt and asked God to shield me from those feelings and help me enjoy the experience of the performance.

This came to my attention when Eloah asked if I wanted to help out with this project. At that time she told me about Deborah's prayer. I thought her thoughtfulness was incredibly cool and said, "You bet . . . count me in."

I played with some great players who were very cool people and some cool players who were great people over the years. I lost quite a number of them to overdoses, gunshots and diseases. Each one I had the pleasure and opportunity to play with, taught me something important. Many said they learned from playing with me too. That's the essence of good music: the give and take of the players communicating; the bass and drums playing off each other; keyboard and lead guitar bouncing lead licks back and forth; vocals giving it personality-horns adding the fill and dynamics-all a big complex balancing act. It takes a good ear, a lot of enthusiasm and finesse to play classy and tasty and to make the group have a sound that gels . . . that's how a trademark sound is born and endures.

I have to say it plain-I had my vices too-maybe more than some. I made sex, drugs and rock and roll part of my lifestyle before there were t-shirts and bumper stickers using the phrase.

For a long time I really liked the buzz from whiskey and other kinds of alcohol. One night after an especially long bus ride, I was offered heroin and I added it to the trio.

Sex was always first chair in the trio; it was a constant-and not always with the most appropriate partners. I loved the ladies and they seemed to love me back—at least for awhile. I had quite a bit of trouble with being faithful. I learned I could love more than one woman at a time. The 50's and 60's had not evolved to modern thinking about morals, behavior and social acceptability to my lifestyle taste. Can't say all my lady partners and wives would agree with me. I made no excuses-it just was what it was. The times were what they were. I made no apologies.

I had to put away the heroin after some years of using, but like any junkie will tell you, you never lose your taste for it. Whiskey doesn't even wash it away. Both were hard-hearted mistresses to ol' Ray.

I had a front row seat for the end of the Jim Crow laws and the reluctant acceptance of integration and the Civil Rights Movement. I met Dr. King and Nelson Mandela and knew many other Freedom Riders and Marchers.

There was such a huge slice of history that occurred during my watch. I didn't get to view it, but was keenly aware anyway.

My God, I went from *"Colored only drinking fountains"* to guys hitting golf balls on the moon to black people in government office as elected governors and senators. My parents would never have imagined such things . . .

I was asked for some advice or helpful tips so here goes:

- **Don't take none of this experience [or yourself] too seriously.** No one gets out alive-that's for sure. This part is the fantasy portion anyway.
- **A sense of humor will get you out of more stressful situations than banging on a Bible or somebody's nose.**
- **Play your mistakes and keep going.** The vast majority of the audience will never know anyway.
- **Look and listen for harmony in all things**; relationships, Nature, music, careers.
- **If you don't know the words, hum.** Fake it 'til you make it. This suggestion fits lots of circumstances.
- **Sing like nobody's listening.** You know how good you sound when you're wailing in the car or shower-don't be timid about expressing yourself. Try many mediums.

- **Be informed not just opinionated.** Know where your belief system comes from. Do your homework and research.
- **God is real. Religion is not real.** Spirituality links Man to God directly, which is how the design was made in the beginning. Interact with God as you would your best friend. If God is not your best friend . . . make it so.
- **Your thoughts are extremely powerful,** be mindful of their direction and content.
- **Your words can wound deeply and leave scars.** Use praise and compliments whenever you can. People hear too little of both.
- **Appreciate people and tell them you do.**
- **Appreciate all you have; thank God for it . . . often**
- **Don't carry grudges;** they get real heavy and slow you down; in fact, the best advice is don't go to bed angry-alone or with someone.
- **Avoid eating meals with folks who upset you or piss you off;** it taints the food you consume and can harm your body. Trust me . . . this is TRUTH!
- **Bless any food, drink, medicine and supplements before you take them** . . . it changes the vibration of the item and helps your body use it more efficiently.
- **"Dance with the one that brung you".** Love God and say thanks as much as you can.
- **Be the best ambassador you can be for God in the world.** It's worth the effort . . . It's the best alliance you'll ever make.
- **It never hurts to be the best dressed one in the room.** Pride stands out from the common herd. A first impression takes 2 seconds to make and lasts a lifetime. Make sure yours is a good one.
- **Be kinder than you need to be.** Everyone has their own struggle going on.

There's lots more I could write, but these are the main ones. Paying attention to these suggestions could smooth out your life, should it get rocky from time to time.

The station you attain in life does not define who you are . . . it's just a measuring stick to see how much you've grown.

If your destiny holds fame, celebrity, notoriety and high levels of success, remember: it's one small slice of a very large pie. It's almost always fleeting and temporary. Fame and celebrity are fickle mistresses.

On the other hand, if you feel you never quite achieved all you thought you could have or should have, you're wasting perfectly good thought energy.

When *woulda', coulda', shoulda'*-the unholy trinity—start to be regulars in your thinking, you need to see it as a call to take action to change your mind. Change whatever starts the chain reaction. Still the voices from the past that start you second guessing yourself. Whoever the voices belong to was just stating an <u>opinion</u>, not God's Divine Truth. **God don't make junk**. You are here 'cause God had a really good idea and like magic there you are!

I know I sound like your preachy old uncle preaching at you, but if my words, thoughts, suggestions, insights, ideas, experience and observations keep you moving forward smoothly on your life path, I can stand to be accused of 'preaching'.

I hope to God, I truly learned from my experiences in my life. I like to think I paid attention some of the time. I hope I was regarded as a good man, caring friend and somebody who really did give a damn about the condition of the world and the people in it. I did my best to give it all I had without holding nothing back in reserve.

I have enjoyed my rest time here in this amazing place. Seeing everybody, [hell-*seeing period*!], catching up, thinking and reflecting. I have a much clearer understanding of choices and events and history . . . and my role in it all. Retrospection was a truly great invention . . . !

Do yourself a favor and do your part like it's opening night . . . not the dress rehearsal the night before. Your time here is precious and it will pass quickly. The opportunities you have to accomplish things that will outlast you are numerous.

Everything is going to be all right in the end. God gave us His promise and, as far as I know, He/They ain't never lied yet.

It's been real . . .

Ray Charles

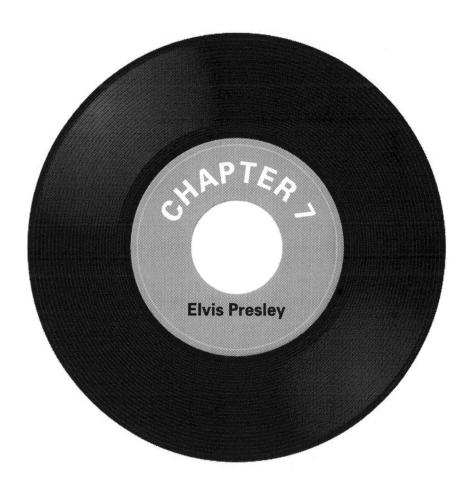

CHAPTER 7

Elvis Presley

Elvis Presley

Hello. My name is Elvis Presley and I've been invited to come by and speak to everyone about God and their amazing world here and the love they have for us.

It's no secret that I have loved the Lord and songs of praise since I was a little boy in Tupelo, Mississippi. I was anxious to go to church services to hear the beautiful music praising God and to join in the singing myself. Learning to appreciate and hear how the harmonies and chords were structured and layered was my musical education. I saw how it moved people.

My family was very poor, but Mama always made sure we prayed over meals and before bedtime. There was no point in arguing or making a fuss—that was her rule of the house.

The details of my early life and background have been written and talked about 'til it's old news, I imagine. Lots of people made lots of money telling their versions of stories about me, my family and friends, my business associates and my career. A few were called to task when the tales just bordered on science-fiction-but mostly everyone got to have their say-their version of "My Life With Elvis", "The King & I" and so on . . . Those of you reading this know exactly what I'm talking about; promoting these products was also an enterprise.

All this body of books, articles and interviews made me a little reluctant to agree to participate in this project of Eloah's. Frankly, I thought maybe people are "over" any influence or remarks I might make. I thought I was maybe yesterday's news. She heard my concerns and pointed out some things that helped me think about all this more clearly.

1. It's a great thing to be able to speak from the heart without anyone from your publicist's office editing every syllable for proper "spin".
2. Much of the publicist's knowledge of me as a man was created by smoke, mirrors and hearsay.
3. My fans made my life and success all that it was and this is my chance to speak to them.

A lot of my life wasn't very pretty. When I could afford to do so, I made it a point to buy my Mama pretty things that made her smile and feel happy-Daddy too. He liked different things than her: he liked toys like I bought for myself-cars, bikes, horses, pool tables, etc. I did all I could to make their later years as comfortable and happy as possible.

My life had some of the most amazing people pass through it-many in the entertainment world, but regular everyday people too. It was necessary that I maintained contact with those beautiful people to keep me grounded and my head on straight when the career was going crazy.

Many of my family and friends are here now. Some were there to greet me as I arrived here. The friendship, loyalty, support and love they brought to my life was appreciated beyond my ability to sufficiently thank them . . . then and now.

My death wasn't pretty either. Nothing glamorous about my coming into the world or exiting either. At the end, I felt bad nearly all the time, never truly slept well, wasn't thinking clearly and I hated looking in mirrors. The man looking back at me was someone I barely recognized and made me sad, depressed and uncomfortable. I used pills to alter all those elements in my life. I thought I could manage all the meds and maintain a delicate balance that my life had become. Those around me who loved me and did have my best interest at heart, tried to intervene, but I wasn't having it. I'd have tirades (in the South we call them "hissy fits") and I had plenty of them! Some of my staff walked away 'cause it got so bad. In my heart I couldn't blame them-they stayed as long as they could-some I chased off . . . not much TLC or TCB involved in that drama.

When I slumped onto the bathroom floor and the separation process of soul from body took place, I hovered over the body that had been my vehicle all those years. It looked so puffy and abused. It felt good to be free and light again. I stayed around for awhile-about 3 days I guess-watching people and their reactions. My death was like truth serum to some. Their true thoughts and feelings came to the surface . . . unfiltered. Very educational I have to say.

Once I began to make my way through the tunnel of light and sound, layers of time, space and dimension-it was mesmerizing—almost hypnotic how the tempo of everything fluctuated. Once I arrived, the welcoming committee was small with just a few familiar faces-Mama in the lead. She hugged me like she would never let me go again-and I let her-and hugged her back just as much. My twin brother was also there; some others you wouldn't recognize, but they were a great sight to see. The whole reunion was low key, quiet and brief. Soon I was being ushered around to meet key people and taking the tour of all that was available. I thought I would feel shy under the circumstances, but I felt quite at home which surprised me 'cause everything is so different than you might think.

My reintegration was brief by etheric standards and everyone I met so exceptionally nice. I sought out some specific entities and a few of them sought me out and came by to say hello and welcome. One of these was Jesus-the Man, not the Christ (a different entity altogether). Jesus hugged me warmly and made me feel immediately welcomed just by his presence. I also met his mother Mary and Jehovah Eloah Vaa Daath (or Mother God) as well as other members of the Elohim (Divine Family).

There's no talking in this place. All conversations are thought transmission. Must say it took me a little while to get the hang of that way of visiting and asking questions, but soon it was completely natural to talk by sending thought images. That's why it is so quiet here-even with all who have assembled.

Jesus asked if I had thought about what I might want to do and He named some possibilities. He then suggested one that really appealed to me: being a greeter for military men and women who arrive. That was what I chose. I did that job for quite some time. I'm told I was a natural for it; that I related well and I could help them feel comfortable in their new surroundings.

One thing you might find funny as you read through these comments: just how many Elvis impersonators ARE there in the world? I can see y'all, ya' know. To be honest, some of them sing better than me. They are a better Elvis than Elvis. The Russian, Spanish, Asian guys . . . at first I wasn't sure *how* to respond to all that scene, then I was reminded by Mama that *"imitation IS the greatest form of flattery . . ."* I pop in and watch sometimes just for kicks . . .

One experience I missed out on was being a granddad to Lisa Marie's kids. I think all those grandparents must be correct about the grandparent experience. I know I would have been over the top indulgent, but I'm told-and I believe-that sometimes too much is just right!

My little angel girl has had an interesting life path with plenty of situations to create challenges for her-some I helped create in her early years. She has a support system to help guide her, but she inherited that wild streak that makes it necessary to experience some things no matter what the cost or consequences.

I think Lisa Marie is a good mother and her experiences will help her assist her children as they try to find and follow their paths.

Her singing and songwriting should be pursued, in my opinion. She has a lot to say and it comes from a distinctive perspective no one else on Earth has.

This might be a good time to address some speculation: I did not "spin" in my grave as some reporters suggested when Lisa

Marie married Michael Jackson. It shocked lots of people, but I knew he genuinely cared for her and loved her to the best of his capability. I think she finally realized that truth after he died and she had time to reflect on many things. His perspective was also unique and I think it made a bond they could have built on-but my sense was the timing was off. There were also some heavy external pressures . . . A different time and place would have had the possibility of a different outcome. Michael and I have had many long visits since he's been here. He is a very loving, caring soul.

As we have freedom to choose what we do with ourselves here, I sing and I listen to others sing and play. There are some heavyweights here to be sure. I can move about and hear different music coming out of every direction.

FYI: Liberace has created his own mini-hall and he plays piano much of the time. He has some folks he helps in the Earth plane, but he has opted to play. He was an old master.

The place where the souls (etheric entities) stay and mingle is called the *Guff*. It's vast and packed with everybody. It's really tough to describe it fully. I think some of the others contained in this book have done better than I could.

I learned-or *RE*-learned-I should say, many of the same lessons other writers have mentioned here.

The things I learned and embraced from church needed to be tweaked and revised to bring them back into Divine Truth. I had never been taught about *The Way*, but here it's all over. *The Way* refers to realizing the scope and magnitude of God's love for all Their children. The phrase *"no greater love . . ."* that's all ya'll gotta keep in mind.

Religious groups have directed lots of folks towards the *"Good News"* instead of *The Way.* They are not interchangeable. The vibration of each is different. Millions of sincere Christian believers are going to be disappointed and disoriented when they realize much of the doctrine they were taught was man-made. Promises that have been made, events that have been foretold . . . it's not going to happen the way so many expect. When this realization shift happens, the upheaval will be a mighty one. Trust God, not man's version of God or his interpretation. God's way and message is much more simple and clear to follow. The truth will march on and prevail and it will make itself known. It's God's words; I just believe what they have stated.

Do I regret or miss anything from the old life? It surprises me that I have full recall of everyone and everything . . . I just think about it all in a different way.

Lisa Marie has called to me in her thoughts many times-even when she was pissed off-and I am always only a thought away . . . always keeping an eye out for her. She has the strength to push through anything on her own power . . . sometimes she needs a confirmation that she's choosing correctly.

Priscilla: I can't sign off without mentioning her. In raising our daughter, managing all the business enterprises, making her own way in the world, 'Cilla has done an exceptional job of stepping up and moving forward. I am grateful to her for more than I ever said to her. A beautiful woman with a good heart and great instincts . . . please accept my apologies.

I've touched on some key points for y'all to consider; if it's not consistent with what you currently believe, then just consider what I've stated here as a "what if" scenario and consider the possibilities.

Take care of yourselves and each other.

Thanks for listening.

Elvis Presley

CHAPTER 8

John Denver

John Denver

Hi everybody . . . John Denver here. It's an honor and a pleasure to be included among so many in this project of Eloah's.

I have had previous contact with Deborah over recent years-mostly visits during meditation at her amazing meditation ranch she created. I asked for permission to visit her there after I had been told some very nice things about her from others here.-principally Stevie Ray Vaughn-but others too. I showed up for a visit and was invited back.

When asked to contribute my impressions to this collection, I wasn't exactly sure what was expected or necessary. Eloah gave the best directive when she simply said "speak from your heart" . . . so I will share from that space.

I really loved so many facets of my earthly life experience. As I grew older, I had a heightened appreciation for Mother Earth and the consummate beauty of all that is nature-especially the Western United States and Rocky Mountains areas. Many of my songs were inspired by the awe I felt just being in and being a part of Nature.

My time with the Cousteau's aboard *Calypso* was especially a thrill for me. It gave me an opportunity to experience the majesty of the ocean and all her inhabitants-great and small: fish or mammal, plant or animal-every bit of it a miracle to behold and appreciate.

No matter where I traveled in the world to perform or lend a hand where I could, I always dreamed of the American West: the mountains and sunsets, elk and buffalo and, of course, all the fascinating people who lived in those areas.

Home was a favorite concept to me. I wrote and sang about it often. Funny thing about 'home', the idea; it's global. It may be universal too, come to think of it. Every language, every culture has a word for it. Everyone knows what 'home' is and what 'home' feels like. It's where you long to be when you're not there and often taken for granted when you are there so you look forward to leaving it . . . especially as a young person. Just can't wait to leave 'home'. Often a journey out into the world makes them appreciate the 'old homestead'-even if it's an apartment somewhere. It's the essence that matters: the energy and the smells-all grounded in Love. That's what drives it-anywhere you go in the world-and now I see from my new perspective; it's truly *all there is*.

I'm pretty good at turning a phrase for a lyric or poem, but I wish I could describe the predominant 'vibe' that is everywhere in this place. All that are here brought their own particular frequency of love vibration with them to be sure, but the love atmosphere of this place defies language. It's one of those things that must be experienced and a thought of the experience transmitted to whomever you are attempting to communicate. At this moment, I am unable to paint a word picture for you who are reading my words here. I am truly sorry about that.

Much of my life experience, like so many others, was a quest for love and to truly come to a point where I felt I could say I had an understanding of it. Of course, a mission like that diverts off to 600 directions because there are so many facets to a love experience.

I am so blessed, fortunate and thankful that my childhood gave me a foundation upon which I could construct the life I did. Moving, marching, exploring, experimenting, recording and remembering what lessons come your way and you take forward in your life journey . . . that's the formula for pretty much anything substantive and worthwhile . . . life, love and music.

74

An important lesson that served me well (and might be useful to you too) was this:

Realize that you are both a teacher and a student in every interaction and relationship you experience in your life.

Everyone can teach you some thing (or things) that are valuable and usable. Of course if you're a teacher worth your salt, you learn at least as much or more from the students than the students do from you. It has to be a universal law of some kind . . . I've seen it to be consistent all over the world.

I'm very grateful for the opportunities I had to travel all over the world to experience and see things first hand. I know it made me a better world citizen, better musician, better man.

Besides being a parent, I will tell you that travelling and experiencing as much of the global diversity that you can would be an excellent goal to set for yourself. It opens up parts of your brain you don't usually activate; it exercises your mind in a good way. But the best benefit-in my opinion—is that it enables you to find out who you truly are as a person occupying space on Mother Earth. I experienced becoming more compassionate, more open to new concepts, ideas and customs; more adventurous in general. Of course, look where that element took me . . . just kidding. [Albeit gallows humor perhaps . . .]

Nature, God, the Universe-whatever label you use-has an expansive capacity for justice and humanity in my experience . . . especially my experience at transition.

When my craft failed and hit the ocean and rocks, the tempo of events really sped up momentarily, then off I headed towards the light tunnel. I wasn't thinking about dying or imagining how the end of my time on Earth would manifest that day. When I was flying and soaring (practically a Zen experience-being at one with the machine and sky) it was really a 'high' in the best sense possible. Soaring with eagles . . . difficult to explain the exhilaration of that experience. It was explained to me later during "re-integration" that my soul agreed that that exact moment would be the one; when my spirit was buoyant with happiness doing something that brought a high degree of joy to me. 'Sorta like the best of a bad situation . . . do you follow my meaning here?

Family and friends-those closest to me—thought flying was very self indulgent and dangerous and I was not exercising good judgment by doing it so much. They didn't understand the healing I experienced and the closeness to nature I experienced when I flew.

I was privileged to have appeared in the *"Oh God"* movie with George Burns. When I first read the script, I really liked how the God character was portrayed; accessible, mystical, clever and witty but lovingly compassionate. George was the perfect actor to play such a part . . . I thought he was amazing. I did have some reservations about how the God character would be received . . . not by the viewers, but by God himself/herself. I did not want to be irreverent or disrespectful. I always thought God had a great sense of humor and I thought it was celebrated in the film. Now my understanding about the essence of God is so much fuller.

When I got here I had a really long list of questions and by getting answers to them, I can say I have a very different and more realistic relationship with the Creator/Elohim.

I found it fascinating that the Elohim love music so much. It's everywhere here and they oversee the creative band of energy that circles the planet. There's been rumors that there might be karaoke night here soon . . . It wouldn't surprise me . . . it would be delightful I am sure . . . ! (kidding).

As a creative energy—or should I say the Ultimate Creative Energy—perhaps they feel a different bond with creative people. They certainly flourish and thrive here, but historically, life in the Earth plane is really taxing on them. It's one of the many reasons they "self-medicate". Earth is a tough gig for a sensitive soul. Alcohol became a preferred escape for me, but I used others as well . . . including sex. I told myself I needed to 'relax' and 'take the edge off', but I have since realized that the adjustment between etheric to earth plane is such a study in contrasts. You put out your music to the audience; something you've spent months crafting, tweaking and rehearsing with your guts and soul in it-and it's promptly panned by the critics or the radio stations won't add it to their play lists. Some songs are just too personal for public consumption, I wrote many I never produced . . . just kept the tracks to myself.

Artists use their gifts and skills to work out challenges in their life path and things they don't understand well-but need to. While all humans walking around have similar challenges, artists do their processing publicly in the glare of the spotlight and media coverage. It makes a guy (or girl) feel very exposed and vulnerable. Their failures and mistakes are stories on the news and in the tabloids. No wiggle room, for sure, but it's part of the package . . . part of the tour you signed up for.

The entertainment business is such a 2-faced business. It has taken the best and brightest and turned them into wood pulp. (Too numerous incidents to count) I think of Elvis and Michael Jackson right away as examples of this. Media darlings then gossip fodder.

If the "hits machine" (i.e. 'the talent') hits a dry spell, it's common, if not standard business practice that they lose their recording contract. That was the circumstance I found myself in. All the hits and appearances, then I had no record deal. I drank more then than I should have and I knew better. It was a huge blow to my confidence as an artist and entertainer and provider, but it was the nature of the business.

It's interesting as I visit with people here, that invariably the question is posed in some form: *"miss anything back there that you left behind?"* Of course I miss my loved ones, but I pop in from time to time to check on their situation, but I miss camping with a fire and the night sky and strumming my guitar, but most of the activities that brought me pleasure I can manifest here . . . just not the people.

My time here has been very enjoyable. I requested a job as one of the coordinators who helps Eloah put etheric artists together with those on the earth plane who agree to channel them. The situations that come up would be a good book for another project . . . !

Crazy stuff—some hilarious . . . some not so much.

Since the Dark Ones have intensified their efforts, screening is more extensive than it used to be—or so I'm told. It's almost like an elevated Homeland Security warning level.

Conversations here are as varied as the participants, but I can tell you there is strong interest and buzz about Jehoshiva's arrival in the Earth plane. Lots of discussion and speculations being put forth about it (but no office pool yet . . .) Elowah will neither confirm nor deny and Jehoshiva himself never goes into any detail about it while he's mingling with folks here. There is much interest here about 'The Way' projects of the Divine Way of Life Center soon to be launched for public exposure. *Keen* interest-lots of people watching.

I've offered some insight and tips I hope will be useful to you as you read through these lines and pages.

In parting I will leave you with these thoughts:

> **Become an expert at forgiveness:** practice and rehearse 'til you are really accomplished at it. It is an art not a science. Be sure to keep yourself at the top of your list of those to forgive. The whole process is a gift only you can give yourself-and when you do, the quality, richness and intensity of your life experiences increases dramatically. Remember: it was a cornerstone of The Way as Jesus taught it. It has withstood the passage of time and has never really gone out of style, but I fear it may become a lost art. When you're really good at something, you make it look easy and others may want to imitate you. As Martha Stewart says: "It's a good thing." Leading by example is still leading.

> **Love God, Love one another, Love Mother Earth**, appreciate what you have available to you and utilize it to the fullest. Be a good steward and ambassador.

As Eloah constantly reminds us: "*You are loved beyond measure and blessed beyond comprehension*"; that's the mantra here. It's also the basis of being an actualized child of God. Relish it, bask in it and grow within it.

Thanks very much for your attention and this opportunity to share.

Much Love to all,
John Denver

CHAPTER 9

Buddy Holly

Buddy Holly

Hello-I'm Buddy Holly. Seems Miss Eloah is partial to Texas folks or those from the South. I told her it reflects her good-make that *impeccable* taste . . . !

It's a thrill to be having my words and thoughts taken down and brought to y'all reading through these pages.

One of the interesting features of this place people may not have stated before, is how time moves. The time it takes you to draw a breath, 50 or 100 years equivalent time could have zoomed past. Blinking your eyes could be a decade. The perception of time is so different when events do not hinge on it like they do in your plane.

When it's noon, the physical part of you has conditioned you to start foraging for something to eat. When it's 1:30 am, your body starts insisting you find a good spot to get some shut eye. Here-aside from no need for clocks-the lack of physical pursuits and requirements make time feel like freefall or free floating. Dimensional fabric is also a factor.

Schedules, waiting in lines, anticipating an event or seeing someone is really very different; all you do is think it and it's occurring. Want to be playing a 9-foot Steinway grand piano? . . . Think you are and you are.

The power of thought energy is celebrated here. It's not something you gotta strive to become adept at, it is the way the place operates.

Sometimes I used to think about young children who pass over to this place. When they're here, their energy is the same as everyone else's. It's not smaller or weaker; it's the same once it's here. A bit of extra processing is needed to achieve that, but there's a system in place to aid that process.

Male and female, old vs. young-all the energy is essentially the same, which makes sense, as the source/origin is the same for all.

I knew very little about spiritual things in my life before I experienced that unfortunate exchange between my plane and the ground. In hindsight, the logistics were very impressive. I had to appreciate the art of it.

The switching of seats, changing minds about priorities, deciding to stay or needing to go-logistically everyone was exactly where they needed to be. Waylon Jennings gave up his seat on that flight and the survivor guilt chewed on him the rest of his life. Once we all met again here, he finally fully understood the whys and the hows-and that it wasn't his time then.

Knowing we were about to crash was the hardest part. We had literally seconds to understand and comprehend we were about to actually D-I-E. We were all young guys-not really emotionally equipped for the events of that night. We were all seeing our dreams being fulfilled, making music, traveling, getting our music out to the kids who made our songs big hits on the radio. We were cocky, but also grateful; thinking we had the world by the tail. We were making a lasting impact on music and the world. We had no idea our deaths would be as famous as our songs.

Reporters wrote that *"Rock n' Roll died that night"* in the Iowa cornfield. In fact, it didn't die, but it seemed to go dormant for a while. Music for the younger set, rock n' roll seemed to flop and flounder around 'til the next big wave hit. Who would have ever predicted it would be a tidal wave from the British Isles!

Each of us pulled some time in the famous 'pink room'-mostly due to the suddenness and shock of the impact. After I was reintegrated, I assumed the job of assisting souls who had cut short their soul contract by taking their own life. You might be tempted to think there would be a lot of judgment here for such people, but surprisingly there is not. Judgment is pretty much limited to critiquing a song you just wrote or a new guitar lick you tried out that somebody just showed you. No judgments to live up to here . . . just opinions.

One aspect of this place that is always intriguing to me is how, as you move about: all the little pockets of music coming from the little groups scattered all over or meeting in specific areas or houses (sometimes halls). It never stops all at once-some people jamming out-not just rock n' roll-but every kind of music ever dreamed about or thought of playing. A famous player is usually playing with an assortment of non-famous and it's all harmonious; most seem to check their egos at the portal door. It would be glaringly obvious were it (the ego) to be evident.

One thing of importance my music career taught me was this:

You gotta listen to the music in your head and guts and reproduce it as closely as possible when you record; the old saying *"to thine own self be true"* was never more important than in the recording studio or onstage. If you ain't feeling it, you'll never be able to sell it to the audience. This is where I had run-ins with record company executives and their hand-picked producers. They had a successful formula for hit records for the label; I had this stream of music in my head that wouldn't shut off. A dilemma to be sure . . . If your music isn't true, you'll never be satisfied when you play it.

I attempted to win them and wow them with my Texas wit and charm, but in the end it was stubbornness that won out. I wore those SOB's down. They said they respected the artistic process, but I knew I was a cash cow to them and they were not doing me any favors—I was saving their company and livelihood and reputations.

Because I stood my artistic ground, my two band members began to think I was setting myself up as king of the outfit. Not my intention at all, but it caused a rift in the band that never fully healed. I was fighting for *us*; for our unique sound, which included *them*. My intentions were misread and hard feelings ensued.

My shining star in my life was Maria Elena, my wife. I really hated leaving her to tour, but it was necessary to promote the records, which generated sales which created paydays for us. She said she understood, but deep down I know it caused her pain-especially when she was pregnant.

I had angels escorting me through the pipeline tunnel after the crash and guides and greeters to receive me once I arrived. I had expectations from my conditioning at church and Sunday school. I remember looking everywhere for a place where there were streets paved with gold! Hey . . . not only no gold, there weren't any streets either! Had to get a quick shot of reality in a hurry . . .

One activity I have enjoyed from here has been to channel through some songwriters to help them craft some good songs-at least in my opinion. I decided I didn't really want another gig on the earth plane-the channeling suited me just fine.

Hope some of this insight is helpful for you.

Later . . .
Buddy H.

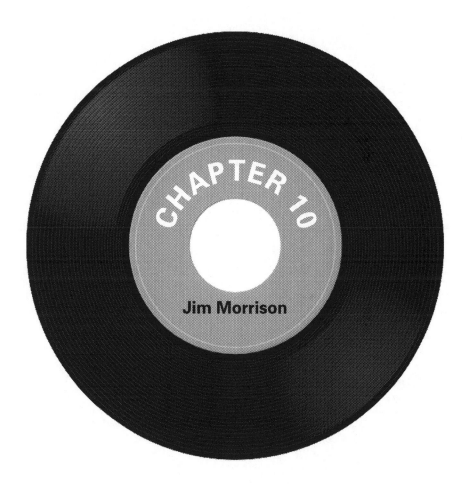

CHAPTER 10

Jim Morrison

Jim Morrison

Hello—I'm Jim Morrison. I was in a band that had some hits and enjoyed some success in the 1960's . . . we called ourselves *The Doors*.

My early life and upbringing was very contrary to what one might expect of a future poet and rock n' roll singer. My dad was a high ranking naval commanding officer and we moved around quite often as his duty station assignments changed. We learned to make friends quickly or not to extend the effort as we would be leaving soon anyway. As my brother and I grew up, we thought this was normal-the only way we'd ever known. As I got older, I soon saw it was a gypsy life without the freedom. My early years were solid for the most part. As you might think, my dad was quite strict when he was there. My mother had a softer approach with us boys, but she was no pushover. They had high expectations for us and very definite codes of conduct that would and would not be acceptable or tolerated.

I got into books and reading early on. Books and the characters that lived within the pages were friends that were consistent as we moved from place to place. Reading helped me learn about words and the power of their meaning. This was most helpful as I began to write poetry and later lyrics to our songs.

Reading helped unlock a part of my mind where the ancient memories were stored; drugs kicked the door open. I would get such streams of consciousness . . . it was sometimes like watching a movie being played in fast forward. It was almost dizzying at times.

Some drugs sped it up and others slowed down the progression so I could take a longer and better look at the images. It was this process that aided my understanding of some of my past lives and the insights to be gained from that understanding.

In the film Oliver Stone made about the band and about me, he got many aspects spot on. His inclusion of the life altering incident regarding the traffic accident of the Pueblo Indians when I was a young boy—about four years old—was portrayed quite accurately. He depicted one of their spirits entering my body and it was unexpectedly correct. I was pleased and somewhat surprised that he included that scene. I would have expected only a small percentage of audience members to understand the significance of that event. Seeing the ancestors dancing with me onstage was also very true. The deeper I looked into the unconscious realms, the stronger my connection to my shaman knowledge became. I channeled a substantial amount of my poetry and lyrics from that place in my soul. There was also a strong link to my lives as a Samurai warrior which gave me access to simplistic vivid imagery in my poetry.

As I bring out my thoughts and words through Deborah by way of channeling, that's very similar to my own experience. Let me say, for certain, this is the only body of work I have contributed to from this vantage point-especially on this topic. I was present for some of the planning and filming of Oliver's picture, but as for written impressions . . . this is it. I stayed close as Val Kilmer worked so hard to get his portrayal of the Lizard King just right. I have assisted Ray Mazarek and some of the others in the studio from time to time, but it was a different vibe and situation.

I was invited to participate in this project by Eloah herself and it feels like a comfortable fit to speak out to all of you good folks reading my words.

Most of my life, I had been reserved, bordering on shy and many people thought I was a 'loner' or 'arrogant' . . . too good to mingle with the minions; all completely false impressions. I observed, learned and wrote about my experiences. I didn't let many people read any of my stuff for a long time; I thought it was too personal. One day it hit me that maybe my writings could be songs. I started to look seriously for some player or players that might be open to collaborating with me. I never aspired to front a band as a singer; in that sense I was truly a 'reluctant rock star', but fate intervened.

When we formed The Doors, it was an interesting time in the music scene in the States. The British bands were dominating the charts and the American bands were trying to find the next new sound that would get traction enough to get record deals and airplay. People were wide open to hear anything new and innovative. If you review some of the albums that were created during those years you can hear it: **Pet Sounds** by the Beach Boys-Brian Wilson just opened up all the channels in his head and this very innovative album came about; and of course, **Sgt Pepper** by the Beatles . . . plus many others. The American sound was heading out of the folk music feel and getting ready to rock out more. The field became wide open for poets and "cellar dwellers" that played for the sheer buzz of making music, to join forces.

Our band had humble beginnings, but our sound had classical overtones, poetic lyrics and a rhythm groove you could move to or trip with.

Once we started getting some airplay and hits, and booking agents were calling us to play, we discovered our freedom to create was being threatened by network censors and label publicists. Everybody was phobic about lawsuits. We held our ground and compromised as little as possible. Maybe you will recall our appearance on the Ed Sullivan Show. We sang *Light My Fire* and they insisted we alter the drug references in the lyrics. They were adamant. We said 'OK' and since it was a live show, I sang the original lyrics-*unaltered*-right into the camera for the folks at home. Sullivan lost his mind and we were banned from appearing on his show ever again.

We didn't set out to be warrior advocates of the First Amendment but we were held up as examples as such.

In Miami, we did a big concert that was later made infamous by my arrest on legal charges based on morality and subjective definitions of pornography and indecency. I was loaded on chemicals and alcohol when I took the stage and I was in a confrontational mood. I admit it: I berated the audience and the police and challenged them on several levels. I got them whipped up into a frenzy mind set and did the "ivory flute" illusion trick. Although no photos were taken as evidentiary proof, I was arrested and taken to jail for public lewdness and indecency and some other lesser charges.

What few people recall was, also in Miami at the same time, the musical "*Hair*" was playing. In it, the cast appears naked on stage while singing. No one was arrested for that public "lewdness" or "indecency". I had money and I got a good lawyer, but the odds were stacked high against me and the authorities were looking for a sacrificial goat and I was designated.

Motions were filed, appearances made, bail was set and I was released from custody. When I got the opportunity, I jumped bail and went to Paris, France where I remained until the end of my life.

Not many details are known about how my life ended; lots of theories and speculation, but not many facts are known.

I will tell you I was very disillusioned by the treatment I received at the hands of the Florida authorities. I accept my portion of blame as instigator and being in an altered state, but felony punishment for misdemeanor offense was overkill . . . and I wasn't the only one who thought so.

In Paris, I spent lots of time with Pamela exploring the city, drank a lot of wine and tried to sort out what strange course my life had taken. I wrote some, but didn't do much. I was hoping to disengage from the rock star facade and reconnect with the poet I knew was closest to my true self. I got fat and lazy in my depression. I grew out my beard so I could change my exterior appearance, while working on the inside. Very early one morning, while soaking in the bathtub after an evening of serious partying with Pam, heart failure occurred and it all came to an abrupt end. My hard living had taken a big toll on my health . . . maybe more than even I realized-though I was cautioned about my excesses on many occasions by friends and business associates, but to no avail. The damage was done in a relatively short span of time. It was accomplished by quantity more than duration as I think back on it. At the end, from Miami to the point of transition, I barely recognized myself in the mirror; all puffed up and bloated. Didn't look like myself. I told several people that I felt I would be the third part of the trinity to die after Jimi and Janis . . . just a feeling that I couldn't shake.

My transition was easy by some standards. I felt like I just let go and started moving through the tube of light and dimension. It was slow at first then picked up speed. I remember not feeling anxiety or fear, just wonder and fascination. I had no thoughts of hell or heaven or God even-I was only focused what was happening at the moment as I went through the process. Once I arrived, I was met by some old friends and relatives and a group of Native American shamen who felt very familiar to me; just a small group with no fanfare. It was like showing up at the back door of a friend's house.

As I made my way through the processing stops, I started to notice I was feeling very different about my life, my purpose-all of it.

I started to realize that my purpose for being here was to contribute to the raising of the collective consciousness that had to happen in the late 1960's; 1969 seems to have been the crescendo of it. I was always pushing against the Establishment-on many levels. I had something to say, I found a means via the music to offer my point of view to the public.

As all life lessons are, it was about love; love of myself and what I had to contribute and love of my fellow man, my brothers and sisters.

Once I got the lesson, no need to hang around re-living the glory days. I just checked out and headed home to the etheric world.

As I had some familiarity with the other side through my visions, dreams and drug trips, I felt more at home than some new arrivals do-or so I was told. My guide was a very old Indian Shaman, Lone White Eagle. When we met up, he embraced me and it was a loving genuine gesture of welcome. I felt it in every part of my being. He patiently and kindly led me around and showed me what I needed to see as well as what options were available to me. I did a short stint in the pink room facility; resolved some anger and disillusionment issues, but that was over quickly and I was soon moving about the 'general population'.

Thinking and communicating with thoughts and pictures and no words was a fascinating process to observe and experience. Makes so much more sense than the Earth way. Communication is much clearer and simple to express one's thoughts, questions, observations and desires.

I meet new people all the time and not all are musicians I choose to spend time with. There were opportunities to meet with the great Indian tribal chiefs like Crazy Horse, Red Cloud, Sitting Bull, Chief Joseph . . . and many others. Their insight and wisdom was mesmerizing to me. They were happy to share their thoughts with me. I also wanted to meet with some historical and political people and I was able to do that. It was very interesting to ask questions and gather insights about historical events and outcomes. One I especially enjoyed was Teddy Roosevelt. He was so knowledgeable about so many things; a delight to visit with him. I've talked to lots of people since I've been here; notable and not, musicians and not, actors, writers, artists and everybody in between. I talked to Marlon Brando for a short time. Fascinating guy; interesting how he looks at the Earth plane process and his role here. On this side, there are others whose names you would recognize . . . but I'm not here to name drop to impress you. You can talk to the same guys I do if you choose to; in meditation. People here have lots of time (as there is none) and love to get invitations to visit with people. You're missing a great opportunity if you don't take advantage of their availability.

Eloah asked that I include some things I've found to be true and pass along to you. I already touched on the transition phase experience and processing, etc.

1. <u>Know your challenges are temporary; try to see into them to find the lesson</u>. Once you learn it, the challenge goes away.

2. <u>Develop the skill, talents and abilities you came equipped with when you arrived</u>. You have them built into your design; not using them is a very foolish choice. Develop and **U-S-E** them as much as you can. Your skill set is one thing that makes you unique in the world scheme of things.

3. <u>Your life is about YOU, but everything else is NOT</u>. If you make yourself the center of your universe, it gets difficult for God and the Divine Family to find seats at the table. Believe me . . . you *want* to have them included!

4. <u>Honor the Earth and don't take it for granted</u>. You are a temporary visitor . . . Mother Earth is here for the long haul. God took a lot of pride in creating the Earth and it is unique in all the Cosmos. Pay attention to how you think about and treat her.

5. <u>Everyone has the ability to affect positive change by their life, example, words and deeds.</u> You never know how you are impacting those around you. Consciously make it something positive and loving. I wasn't very effective at this. I knew better, I just didn't do it like I should have.

6. <u>Be a friend to yourself</u>. Nurture and support your own choices, fears and challenges. If you do this, you'll be a better friend and companion to others.

7. <u>Stand in truth</u>-not just your version of what you think the truth looks like. Truth is what it is. It has power and energy. It can be a sword and a shield. Whenever there is doubt—use TRUTH.

8. <u>Acknowledge your connection to God</u> or whatever term you use to refer to the Creator. Acknowledge, embrace

and develop it to the best of your ability; in the beginning, the middle and the end, it's really all there is. God's name is Love; God's nourished by the love we give back; it's all about Love in its purest form. Get immersed in the idea and energy of it all. If this seems foreign to you, you've forgotten what your unconscious knows to be true. Meditate and get back in touch with your own knowing of God. God is the core of all things. You cannot truly love anything or anyone if God is excluded from the equation.

9. Appropriate your time to cover important things. Your time on the Earth plane is brief by any standard; utilize it to the fullest, explore and experience all you can while you're here. The opportunities to do so are unique to this place. Don't waste time while you're here.

10. Leave a good story behind when you leave. The Native American tradition is to tell of one's exploits and accomplishments in stories around the campfire. What kind of story is told about you after you leave is completely up to you. You shape it day by day . . . decision by decision. People will probably not remember your words, but they will always remember how you treated them. Decide on the legacy you want to leave behind and set about to create it now day by day.

11. Learn all you can about everything you can. You'll be more interesting, you'll have a better understanding of how the world works and don't forget . . . it's all recorded in your unconscious.

12. Don't live in a constant state of altered consciousness. If you have to drink every day or smoke a joint before you leave the house-[hell, even coffee alters your mood]-you're missing a lot. Sometimes you must be straight and sober to feel things and understand certain situations, etc. *LaLa Land* is not a good place to live. This may sound strange from me, but that's how I know for sure it's true. Life is painful and

uncomfortable sometimes. Those things are great teachers. If you medicate yourself to a flat line with no highs and lows, my God, think of all you let pass you by! Isn't experience why you came here?

13. <u>Express yourself; however and whenever you can</u>. Sing, dance, write, make people laugh, entertain a little child, do artistic projects, organize the world's spice rack . . . When you do, you make a difference in the world.

Thanks to Eloah and Deborah for letting me add a bit to this cool project. Thanks to all who have been reading our words. If they were not Divine Truth Eloah would not let them be included.

Shine brightly,
Jim

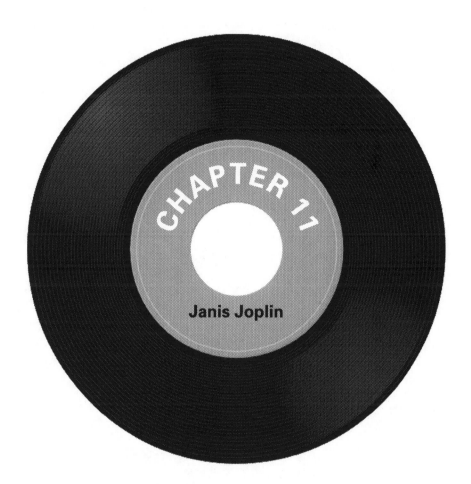

CHAPTER 11

Janis Joplin

Janis Joplin

Hey . . . I'm Janis Joplin from Texas; got an invite to share my thoughts and experiences with y'all by Eloah.

I used to sing the blues. Folks said I sang them like nobody else; like the feeling was coming from my bones not just my soul and heart.

The day I decided to sing was the day that saved my life. I started out singing all kinds of music; country, folk, etc.—depending on the gig. But here's the thing: *singing helped me find my voice—* funny, huh?

I tried to make myself fit into lots of situations in my younger life; daughter, sister, student, girlfriend . . . and later singer. Problem was, I didn't fit into the folks' expectations. I felt I was constantly letting them down, disappointing them—mostly myself. Some people even told me how I had let them down . . . some just let it hang unspoken in the air between us.

There were a few who were trusted enough to be close to me-especially my sis. Whatever was transpiring in my life, I tried to keep in touch with her . . . letters from the road and sometimes by phone.

Austin, Texas was a good memory for me. As I got established there, I made some friends, some noise and some music-folk mostly. It was a good place to develop my pipes and to test the waters to see what music suited my voice best. Threadgill's (café & bar) was my home away from home for some time. Lots of good experiences gained from appearing there. Lots of love to those great folks . . . now and always.

Moving to California was stressful and exciting at the same time. It was cool 'cause I could re-invent myself. I had no history only what I wanted to tell people about myself. That's where *Pearl* got some recognition . . . like my alter ego. Pearl could be sweet, but she sometimes had to be hard as nails too.

Much of what came my way was overwhelming sometimes. The physical demands of performing and traveling all the time, loneliness, failing relationships-man, it all tore at me . . . really deeply affected me. Alcohol lightened and loosened me up so I could perform onstage, but the same situations were still there waiting for me when I stepped off the stage; soon even Southern Comfort wasn't keeping the demons at bay well enough.

I was offered heroin at a pre-stage party one night and I really liked having all my life issues suspended for awhile; I felt light and airy like a young girl again. I kept using. I know I danced close to the edge many times . . . by myself and with others . . . but I always came back.

After I'd been in the music biz for awhile, the demons of the past: insecurities, fears, acceptance . . . the whole thing seemed to grow bigger and harder to subdue. The new thing of fame and celebrity also added to the mix . . . more expectation.

I sang with great bands and performed at some really huge events that became historical-like Woodstock, Monterey and others. Unfortunately, I couldn't remember much about those experiences. I watched films of my performances and it was like an out of body experience seeing myself. The *'me-thing'* I noticed was the booze and junk took the lid off my inhibitions and all the raw emotions came flooding out in my voice. It was like the pain I kept bottled up inside erupted out unchecked. People called it powerful, soulful blues . . . but it was the energy of my soul processing my inner pain. Did I know all this at the time? No way! That knowledge came later after I made transition. Like some of the others have said earlier, you are too engulfed and distracted by your earthly life experience and you forget some of the reasons you came here in the first place. It's easy to do; really hard to climb out of the routine.

I thought success and money would be the great equalizer . . . maybe make up for looks, popularity, relationships that never succeeded, acceptance and acknowledgement. What it really did was widen the gap I felt between me and other people; plus I had to decide if they liked me or my supposed "status". It really fueled my loneliness and feeling of separateness.

The one thing success _did_ bring was this: for awhile-while I was onstage pouring my guts out in a song list-I really did experience love energy focused on me from the audience. It was the best buzz and high of all . . . way better than any drug or booze . . . but it didn't last. When the show was over, so was the buzz. It was an addiction of a different sort. Lots of performers can describe how it affects them. It's different for everybody; people have their own versions of insecurities, fears, and so on . . . and the "_audience jones_" feeds each of them differently. The lows are very low and the highs are very high. The middle ground is just scary and uncomfortable.

This was really brought home to me when I decided to make a grand entrance and attend my high school reunion in Port Arthur, Texas. I arrived in a limo and dressed in full rock regalia and got laughed at—again . . . still. I left and never looked back. I had hoped those who never accepted me during the school years, would somehow have changed their attitude towards me. Well, they did . . . **it got worse!** Deciding to return for that reunion was the best and worst decision I had made in a while. _Good_ in that it removed all hope and delusion of being accepted by the hometown folks and _bad_ in that it really wounded me. Knowing that I had changed and still couldn't fit in; and why did I still _want_ to?? It ended a lot of delusions and what—ifs, hopeful/wistful thinking . . . all in one brief social outing. I did look good, though, at that damn reunion! I let Pearl take center stage for that appearance.

Being a Texas girl from a small town, I had been taught about God at Sunday school and Church. Funny how those ideas stick and stay with you into adult life-even when you think you're ignoring them.

When I was puking my guts out or sick from needing more drugs or 'cause I had taken too much, did I pray? Damn right I did. I made deals, begged and pleaded to get through the immediate situation at hand. I would get through it and I'd forget about the promises I made.

Funny thing about God as I have since come to understand and know how they operate: They weren't going to let me go; they kept me tethered to them through <u>everything</u>. They were my soft place to land in the hardest times of my life. I knew it on the deepest levels, but consciously I was too engaged in the physical journey. Like so many, and as it's been stated by others in this book, it's easy to get consumed by the physical trip your soul is taking; which is exactly opposite to what the perception is: *you are not a physical being on a spiritual trip; you're a spiritual being on a physical trip.* If you view it any way other than the Truth, it will really confuse you. I lost track of it and got lost in the shuffle of events. I started feeling trapped in my life and I found out later, I had the power to change *all* the circumstances. The outcome was set by my Divine contract, I made it harder than it had to be . . . it's choices and perception, man! You start feeling that you're alone-not connected to God. Once you go there in your mind, things get much tougher to cope with day by day.

There wasn't much in my life that I would call 'pretty' and my death scene wasn't either. I had completed my journey and my contract was fulfilled. It was time to go back to the etheric world-so I did.

The process was much like has been discussed here by my colleagues. I won't re-hash all they've already described. I will say it was very interesting and not scary at all. I remember thinking: *"Wow, lots of my life was way more scary than this trip!"* I saw quite a few musician friends when I got here and, of course, family members too, not a ticker tape parade . . . more like a reception-like trip. Nice . . . kinda' subdued . . . it was all good. Had a little time in the famous "pink room suite"—then out and about.

I opted to take a job counseling people as they draft their contracts for coming back to Earth. I help them with logistics and outcomes and language; all really important. Turns out, I'm pretty good at this work. Helped lots of people.

Occasionally, Eloah brings to my attention some young artist that might be compatible with my new and improved energy and I get to channel through them for a performance or even a song. It's fun, but I don't have the pain to put into the song anymore. I can still sing the blues, I just don't have a heart full of them anymore.

I am loved completely and I feel it! I am accepted completely and all my other fears and issues are gone. It's fabulous!

As others have been asked to list some important lessons— here's mine:

1. **Know who you are and don't let the opinion of others derail you from loving, liking or accepting yourself-** however you look, feel or are TODAY. It will all change tomorrow anyway.

2. **Find an emotional anchor you can trust and use them to help keep yourself grounded.** A friend or family remember might work for the Earth plane; use one of the Divine Family or all of them for Spiritual grounding.

3. **If you don't feel comfortable in your life circumstances, use your power to change it**. You are more powerful than you realize. Remember who your Divine Parents are and go with that. Ask for their assistance-they will love to help but cannot until you ask them to do so.

4. **Be nicer to people than you are required to be**. You make better memories for yourself and others by following this principle.

5. **Forget trying to be "perfect".** Mistakes teach us far more than perfection. Be flexible, adaptable and open to learn; that's the best you can hope for and stay sane.

6. **God's there to assist-not inflict harm.** Learn this as early as possible. Lots of energy wasted on blaming God for stuff and being angry at God. Absolutely no point to it . . . ZERO!

7. **Accept responsibility for your bad choices and judgement calls.** When you screw up, embrace it, bless it and move on. Refer to #5. Screwing up is a great way to learn.

8. **Allow people the pleasure of helping you.** You are not an island, you're a social creature. Sometimes it's a big blessing for others when they can help you. Allow them this pleasure; it's a blessing for you too.

9. **Let yourself be loved**. By God, by your friends. Know you are lovable and accept it when it's offered. Love isn't perfect, it's just what it is. Embrace it and *accept* . . . it's the best gift possible.

10. **Love others as much as you can.** Love God first, then your neighbor as yourself-the rest works itself out.

My life wasn't perfect and my ideas aren't either, but what I've shared with you is what I know to be Truth in the Divine Way. Some I gained from retrospect, some from my reorientation when I arrived here in the etheric plane. If it was not correct and accurate, it would not be permitted in this collection of essays . . . this I know for sure.

Learn, laugh, love and grow every day-do something good in the world today.

God bless y'all ___

Janis J

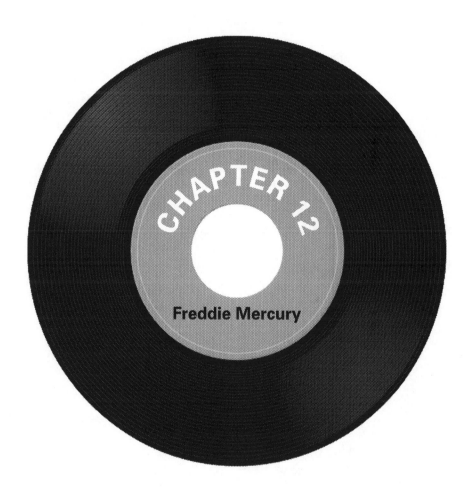

CHAPTER 12

Freddie Mercury

Freddie Mercury

Hello My Darlings; it's Freddie Mercury speaking. I am most grateful to have this opportunity to express my thoughts and experiences again.

There have been so many shows, articles, books, etc. produced about Queen; the individual members and myself . . . globally so; for some reason I found it to be odd somehow. I know our popularity was worldwide, but until one tours extensively and witnesses the fame firsthand, it remains abstract and difficult to absorb-much less comprehend. In Russia and other Eastern bloc countries, all of Asia, South America, Australia and (to a lesser degree) America, we saw stadium size venues sell out time and time again and tens of thousands of people pay to have a Queen experience and sing along. Even when the language was totally alien to them, they still knew all the lyrics and soon I grew to think of it all as a common language we all spoke and understood. It was extraordinary.

Music made so many parts of my life possible and I feel I owe a great debt to the 'music gods' . . . not to say I did not work incredibly hard-as did we all-to achieve the level of performance and excellence we ultimately came to be known for: versatility, adaptability-always stretching and reaching to re-invent ourselves. I think our audiences liked not knowing what direction we would lead them next.

My instructions to participate in this project were quite minimal: *"Speak your truth, say it in love and share your experiences as you wish."* I asked to be included and Eloah was so gracious to permit me to do it.

My tale is somewhat different than many of my fellow contributors to this body of work. I didn't die suddenly or unexpectedly. I had the gift of time to say what needed to be said, get my business and personal legal matters in order and to reflect in the quiet hours when pain or medication did not permit me to sleep or work. It is some of these thoughts I decided to share here. I thank those of you reading or hearing this for indulging me.

My personal philosophy and introduction to spiritual beliefs was quite unique because of traveling and living in different countries with varied cultures and customs. My exposure to different religious beliefs and practices left me more open-minded than many of my peers or friends in the various levels of schools I attended. I also read many books on all sorts of topics as I was growing up. I was frequently *"the new kid"* in school, often the *"odd guy out"* who seldom fit into any of the cliques all schools seem to have. I looked different and was somewhat introverted as a young boy; later I was experimenting with various ways to express this very strong "inner push". I had to <u>do more</u> and <u>be more</u> and later that experimentation phase would evolve to *"wild and reckless abandon"*.

I always had dreams that gave me a wealth of information; glimpses of both my past and future, creative inspiration, options when I had important decisions to make; some I spoke of and most I kept private. These dreams always seemed to set the bar very high for me . . . like I was expected or destined to grow into what they foretold; they tugged and pulled me in directions and towards heights of achievement that were certainly not the norm for musicians and bands when we started playing as students. There was the added pressure on me as the "production manager of dreams" to get the boys in the band to share my vision and make the necessary changes to go with what I was seeing in my head. Sometimes it was difficult, sometimes not . . . sometimes my band mates thought I was difficult or a control maniac. To be fair, many times that was a fair assessment. I was blessed with a healthy ego, but to achieve grand goals, one has to think in grand terms-be it theatrical stage production, song/vocal arrangements or social or lifestyle choices. It was necessary to think in 'larger than life' terms. Many people passed through my life like a revolving door at times-because they just never understood that basic fundamental basis of my view on my life and work.

I had several very glorious and flamboyant past lives that afforded me the opportunity to be a performer and be in the public eye in various roles and endeavors. As everyone does, I also had non-descript, mundane, ordinary type lives as well. I know for certain I drew upon many of my collective life experiences for inspiration and guidelines for managing some of the craziness that comes from fame and celebrity.

As Farouq, I was born with a large stock of talent and gifts of various sorts, but also challenges that had to be met and overcome to develop my talents and skills so I could implement my dreams.

I always knew we would be hugely successful; no real doubt about it in my mind and gut . . . selling it to the boys, managers, club owners, etc. was harder.

Due to the time element, I decided early on-when I knew I was ill-not to hand over control of my life to the disease. It was my enemy and I decided to fight 'til I couldn't fight any longer. I accomplished that goal. I didn't dwell on it or discuss how I felt . . . I refused to put any life force energy the direction of the disease. I channeled every bit of energy possible towards work: writing, recording tracks, making videos and performing as long as possible. Touring and concert dates were the first to go; after that I focused on studio tracks.

During this time I did pray-most often for strength and endurance or a pain level that was manageable. I did get the assistance I requested. I had a small, elite support group that was unwavering in their love and support. It was small by my own design and choice as I kept my illness on a 'need to know' basis up until the very end. I hope I adequately conveyed to them how much they were appreciated and treasured.

My transition was smooth and as I describe it to you now, it felt "well orchestrated". I remember not feeling fear-mostly tired and heavy, then relief! Lots of sensations went along with actually releasing and moving through the dimensional layers to reach the etheric part of the world.

Mostly-by a huge majority-people have the completely wrong idea about dying. No one I knew had it right . . . guess it's all supposition up to a point. It's definitely one of those experiences where *"you had to be there"*. A postcard just doesn't do it justice!

Let me tell you, it's not a dreadful, scary experience. Most of what people think comes from books, pulpits and movies, I'm sad to say. It sets a negative tone for the process as a whole. I could feel my soul essence as it began to disengage from my failing and frail physical body. Once I was 'out of body' as it's described so often, the body functions soon systematically ceased to work. I felt two beings that I now know were angelic beings who each took me by the arm and supported and guided me through the long walkway that was lined with brilliant flashes of colored lights that were moving as we moved through them. In the distant background, I caught a glimpse of and had an awareness of a star field-like space with tiny points of lights.

Once the walkway was finished, we entered a gigantic chamber-type enclosure that felt cool, but was filled with warm, yellow gold energy. It was here I saw some familiar faces: friends and family. As I moved about, I felt very self aware; my hands and face had a translucent glow emanating from them. I felt an odd, intense electric-type tingle during this journey through the walkway. Once on the other end, what I experienced was quite similar to what other accounts shared in this book described. I had minimal time in the pink room so many have mentioned . . . actually quite a smooth trip, all things considered.

I have had and enjoyed many long visits with Eloah and others of the Divine Family. I had quite a few questions and Eloah was most gracious and generous with Her knowledge and spending large blocks of what's called 'time' here. I did not have an awareness of Her until I arrived here. I was never taught anything about the existence of a Mother God in school and can't recall any discussions that referenced such an entity. It's a shame that most people have no awareness of her important role in the complete timeline of planet Earth and mankind. Lots of fascinating people have approached me and initiated great conversations . . . like the ultimate orientation mixer at college.

Here's some information I can pass along that you might find useful—or at least interesting:

You can be assured you are *never* alone. Someone in some form is always able to watch/observe you . . . in a positive, protective way. They cannot intervene unless expressly invited to do so. Your free will makes you a sovereign being so if you want their assistance you must make your wish known.

Grudges and fears don't make the trip. My experience was these were left behind. Only the warm and fuzzy emotions carried forward. The thoughts were there, the negative emotions attached to the thoughts were gone. Knowledge remained, none of the emotions used to acquire the knowledge.

Angelic beings are too beautiful to adequately describe in usual language. It's hard to not stare at them while being unable to speak. Artist renditions don't do them justice.

Don't back away from dreaming big dreams for yourself. Destiny's a powerful force. Trust it. If your life journey must wind and course to bring you to destinations, situations and circumstances you need to accomplish what you must, know it's going to happen somehow. My own life is a perfect testament of this truth; coming from very obscure geographic beginnings and look at all that happened to maneuver and prepare me for each phase of my life journey. Remarkable really . . . how the logistics come together. Proof positive of the orderly nature of the universe as it affects each of us.

Religion is man-made and not even close to being Divine Truth in most facets and applications and it's not *nearly* as interesting. Everyone who chooses to establish a one-on-one relationship with the Power greater than themselves whatever name they assign to *It*—has a huge advantage in every way possible as they have their earth experience. This relationship falls under the classification of *spiritual* instead of *religion.* The basic difference is simple as this: <u>Spiritualism</u> is a connection directly between you and God; <u>Religion</u> uses a person (pope, priest, clergy, pastor, etc.) as the intermediary between you and God.

<u>Y</u>our time is fleeting; it goes by quickly. I hope you will stuff as much loving, living, experiencing, experimenting as you can possibly manage, leaving a positive legacy in your wake. Life is a wonderland; experience all that you possibly can . . . oh yes, and darlings, it doesn't hurt to be *fabulous* while you're busy living large. You don't need to be wealthy financially to accomplish this directive . . . use your imagination, creativity and recruit your amazing friends to help inspire and execute your most fantastic adventures and excursions.

Love who you love and make sure they know how much you treasure and appreciate them being in your life. Old friends, new friends, work friends, family members, lovers . . . anyone who loves you, tells you the truth, makes you laugh, keeps you grounded . . . embrace them literally and figuratively . . . all ways you can so they always know how you feel. This is a life imperative. Assuming they know and never saying it doesn't work in the long run. Taking their presence for granted or making them feel taken for granted is a very negative component for a great relationship.

Well, I feel I have prepared you for launch . . . I hope YOU feel ready! Now get busy . . . off you go . . . !

Be brilliant in all things . . . and be sure to dance on the edge,

Forever,
Freddie